INTIMACY IN ALCOHOLIC RELATIONSHIPS

A Collection of Al-Anon Personal Stories

Al-Anon Family Groups

Help and hope for families and friends of alcoholics

For information and a catalog of literature write to:

Al-Anon Family Group Headquarters, Inc.
1600 Corporate Landing Parkway
Virginia Beach, VA 23454-5617
(757) 563-1600   Fax (757) 563-1656
al-anon.org   wso@al-anon.org

Al-Anon/Alateen is supported by members' voluntary contributions and from the sale of our Conference Approved Literature.

Library of Congress Control Number: 2018941350

ISBN 978-0-9995035-1-5

Approved by
World Service Conference
Al-Anon Family Groups

Al-Anon books that may be helpful:

Preamble

The Al-Anon Family Groups are a fellowship of relatives and friends of alcoholics who share their experience, strength, and hope in order to solve their common problems. We believe alcoholism is a family illness and that changed attitudes can aid recovery.

Al-Anon is not allied with any sect, denomination, political entity, organization, or institution; does not engage in any controversy; neither endorses nor opposes any cause. There are no dues for membership. Al-Anon is self-supporting through its own voluntary contributions.

Al-Anon has but one purpose: to help families of alcoholics. We do this by practicing the Twelve Steps, by welcoming and giving comfort to families of alcoholics, and by giving understanding and encouragement to the alcoholic.

Suggested Preamble to the Twelve Steps

Serenity Prayer

God grant me the serenity
To accept the things I cannot change,
Courage to change the things I can,
And wisdom to know the difference.

Contents

Preface

Since as early as 1954, Al-Anon members have been asking for written material about sex and alcoholism. In 1955, our first book, *The Al-Anon Family Groups* (B-5), responded to these requests somewhat tenuously with a chapter titled "The Sex Problem." It was about the same length as this preface.

As our membership grew to consist of other relationships besides the wives of alcoholics, the requests continued, but they now extended beyond the topic of sex and marriage to encompass intimacy in all its many forms, including emotional, physical and spiritual.

Unfortunately, every attempt made over the last 60-plus years to include the topics of sex and intimacy in Al-Anon's Conference Approved Literature was hindered to some extent by the same component that makes our literature unique and powerful—that it is written by our members. Members have wanted to read about sex and intimacy, but have often been very reluctant to share. As one member stated, intimacy is "the *real* 'elephant in the room.'"

And yet, recommendations for literature about intimacy have continued, including one brought by the Literature Committee to the 2011 World Service Conference, Al-Anon's largest representative group conscience. Conference members enthusiastically embraced the idea of a new piece of literature encompassing a wide variety of relationships, situations and experiences with all types of intimacy. They felt this piece could include sexual intimacy without focusing exclusively on it, and agreed to "give conceptual approval for a new piece of literature on intimacy in general, including sexual intimacy, in alcoholic relationships." But even in carrying the motion, the Conference wondered if enough members would send in sharings to make production of the piece possible.

Though the response was gradual and took time, eventually over 1,300 members willingly shared their stories. They told how their views and practices of intimacy, including sexual intimacy, were affected by alcoholism, and how Al-Anon's tools and spiritual principles helped them change these views and practices. We are extremely grateful to these courageous members, whose thoughts, feelings and experiences have been compiled into *Intimacy in Alcoholic Relationships*, and hope that as a result, many other members can find hope and inspiration in expanding their recovery.

Intimacy in Alcoholic Relationships

Chapter One
Alcoholism and Intimacy

When confronted with the idea of intimacy, many of us stop short. We balk at the notion of discussing such an uncomfortable, sensitive subject, even within the relative safety of the Al-Anon program. It is not a terribly common topic for a meeting, so unless we're participating in a Fourth Step study or attending a workshop, we may never have considered speaking about intimacy in a group setting. Even the thought of sharing one-on-one with a Sponsor or another trusted Al-Anon friend may give us pause.

And yet, the need is there. Many of us feel like we are outsiders, permanently separated from everyone in our lives, even from our fellow Al-Anon members. We yearn to connect with other human beings, but have no idea how to do it. Discovering how to form and maintain intimate relationships in every aspect of our lives is crucial to our recovery. If we cannot feel like we are "a part of" instead of "apart from," we may never leave behind the feelings of isolation that are such a debilitating effect of the disease of alcoholism.

For many of us, the word "intimacy" conjures thoughts of sex, and not much more. Whether we grew up affected by the disease of alcoholism, or were affected later in life, admitting the subject of sex into our minds may seem impossible—or at least impossibly uncomfortable. We may have acquired the notion that sex is dirty, a taboo, never to be mentioned in polite conversation, or any conversation at all. For those of us who have experienced sexual abuse or molestation, thinking about sex can be painful or terrifying, and it may seem safer to avoid the topic—and maybe sex itself—altogether. Others of us may have thrown ourselves into sexual relationships without much thought, and may hesitate to examine our attitudes around sex, for fear of rocking the boat.

While intimacy is certainly a necessary component to a healthy sexual relationship, sex is not its full extent. Intimacy, as we come to learn in Al-Anon, is not exclusively sexual, but rather includes feelings of closeness, safety, connectedness and trust. Each of us may experience intimacy in our relationships with others, with ourselves, and with our Higher Power. Something as simple as giving and receiving hugs at the end of a meeting can help us form a powerful connection with others.

The effects of alcoholism, however, can stand between us and others, affecting our ability to experience closeness in relationships in a healthy way. Here are some perspectives that members have shared about intimacy:

- "At one point after my divorce, I honestly believed that it was my spiritual destiny to be alone."

- "I thought that if I had sex with these men, I could somehow get them to love me and stay."

- "I used to believe that making love began early in the day, with a glance exchanged, a kiss or caress, with more as the day went on. Now the slurred speech, repetition of thoughts and smell on his breath turn me off totally."

- "While I freely gave of myself physically, I withheld my emotions and my vulnerabilities."

- "We used to sleep so entwined it was hard to move. Now we each seek our side of the bed and if we accidentally touch, we jerk away."

- "I never gave anyone my whole self. I was intimate with no one. I felt like I was not worth knowing."

- "In order for me to have any relationship, I thought it was necessary to cover up, lie (by omission) and be grateful for any crumbs I got."

- "Extreme modesty was the norm in my family of origin, and even the 'birds and the bees' talk I got before I started dating lasted about one minute."

- "As a teenager I was very afraid of my father's sexuality because while he drank, he would make sexual advances toward my mother. My fear was that, while drunk, he would mistake me for my mother."

- "We moved frequently. I gave up on making friends early on. I was lonely. I eased my painful isolation with food and reading."

- "We never got hugs and I don't remember being held. I do remember pretending to be asleep after a car ride, so my dad would have to hold me in his arms and carry me in the house. I think now that I craved that physical affection."

With so many barriers to intimate relationships, how can we begin to overcome the damage wrought by alcoholism in our lives? Certain program tools may spring to mind when we consider examining the problem of intimacy. A Fourth Step inventory can be particularly helpful. We might choose to work the sections on "Love," "Intimacy" and "Sex" in *Blueprint for Progress* (P-91) individually with a Sponsor or other Al-Anon friend. We could attend a Fourth Step meeting or a workshop on intimacy at a District or Area level event. No matter how we approach it, a careful examination of our experiences and attitudes—past and present—regarding intimacy can be illuminating, and essential to our recovery.

Members Share Experience, Strength and Hope

I never let myself get close to people

I always equated the term "intimacy" with adult sexual situations. It wasn't until I had been in Al-Anon for a while that I realized that intimacy can refer to huge parts of my life that have nothing at all to do with sex. I learned a new definition and, with that insight, realized I had almost no intimacy with friends, God, my Sponsor or even myself.

It's only because I am practicing being more vulnerable and real in my Al-Anon groups that I can recognize how distant I've always kept people from me—regardless of how close in physical proximity. In school, people thought I was popular and had a lot of friends, but what I really had were a lot of acquaintances. It was like I had a bubble around me. The few I considered close friends were still held at arms-length. Of course, I wasn't aware of any lack of intimacy—I thought it was normal and as close as everyone else got with each other. I don't think my parents had emotional intimacy with each other, or with me, even though they worked hard to keep up a front of family closeness in pictures and family visits.

I have become much more intimate with God through Al-Anon and I think this has given me the courage to try it with friends, my Sponsor and my husband. I have been genuinely surprised at how un-vulnerable I still am with people in general. I think intimacy and sex issues are a big part of the results of being affected by alcoholism. It's a hush-hush topic that I'm glad to see is becoming more open for discussion.

My distorted thinking contributed to the problems in our marriage

Intimacy: I have such a deep desire to experience it, yet I am also very fearful of it. I have a strong desire to experience intimacy physically, emotionally and spiritually. I desire to allow someone to see who I really am, while trusting that I will be accepted and supported. I desire to be in a relationship where I feel safe to be naked—literally and figuratively—and still be accepted in spite of the imperfections I reveal.

I did not grow up in a home where I learned how to share who I was, and so I had limited skills and ability to reveal myself to someone. Perhaps it is no surprise that I married a person who also had difficulty being intimate. Maybe in an ideal world we each could have trusted each other enough to work on the issues and become intimate. Unfortunately, her growing dependence on and abuse of alcohol introduced serious obstacles to achieving that possibility.

The alcoholism led my partner to cover up, hide and lie about who she was. My trust disappeared. My response, before coming to Al-Anon, did not include acceptance of this as being part of a disease, nor was I able to support her in an effective manner. Rather, I saw alcohol as her desired primary relationship, and that I was at best a distant second. I no longer felt like an important part of her life and began to distance myself emotionally. It was easy to justify withdrawing emotionally and not sharing myself, believing it was not emotionally safe to do so. In some ways it wasn't, but I believe it also allowed me to avoid my fear of being intimate and vulnerable.

As the drinking progressed, I began to notice that she seemed to find me more physically attractive after she had been drinking. Later I learned this behavior had its roots in her being abused by a male neighbor when she was young. At the time, however, I interpreted this to indicate that I was basically undesirable and that I only became desirable after her mind was clouded and her body numbed with alcohol. I began to wonder if, in that state, any male body would suffice. My weak self-esteem took a serious blow. In my crazy thinking, I removed my wedding ring, justifying this action because I believed her primary love was now a bottle of vodka. I thought I was making a statement about how serious I believed alcohol was damaging our marriage. Much later I learned how much this hurt her, and how very damaging this act was to our marriage.

We were unable to develop closeness at a spiritual level. We grew more emotionally distant as a result of alcoholism and my response to its unwelcome presence. The steadily growing emotional distance led to a growing physical distance. The physical touching became much less frequent and after several years our relationship became asexual. I longed to touch her and to be touched, but my fears, hurt and anger gradually replaced the joy and pleasure. I found it difficult to be physically close while being so emotionally distant. Rather than being a pleasurable expression of love, sex became a risky encounter. I occasionally thought about how male spiders mate with a female and then try to escape becoming dinner. My thinking was very distorted. Now that I'm in Al-Anon, I understand how my reactions to this extremely difficult situation made circumstances worse.

I am learning I am lovable

I grew up with alcoholic parents who seemed to hate each other. They were vicious, violent and spiteful. My dad was away working a lot of the time. I discovered recently that when I was little, he had another secret house with a secret girlfriend in it. He was always unfaithful to Mum and talked about her—even in front of her—saying how unattractive and stupid she was. My mum was seething with bitterness, which seeped out at every moment. They had fistfights and broke the china. They also directed their anger at their children.

I discovered that boys were a good escape. I didn't want sex, as a young teenager. I was too insecure about my body and felt too damaged already, but I loved the safety of being with someone. I loved that feeling of being wanted—even for a little while, or at least the illusion that someone was protecting me—even if they reluctantly let me tag along because I had run away from my dad who was going to punch me. I lost my virginity on a day when I had stayed away from home because I was frightened to be there. My boyfriend said I had to, so I did. I remember crying all the way through and hating my boyfriend for making me. I caught him kissing another girl two weeks later. I pretended not to have seen them, but just drifted away and didn't have contact with him anymore. I could see I was nothing special to him.

I never expected to be special to anyone. I slept with a lot of men in my teens, twenties and thirties. I made myself an expert in performing sex. I thought if I could impress a man with my talent, that it gave me worth and made me memorable. I thought I had to push out my boundaries to please men. I always slept with them as soon as they wanted and probably sooner. I slept with a lot of men I was not even attracted to because I thought I was supposed to, because I didn't know how to say no and because I was so desperate for attention and affirmation that I was wanted—on any level at all.

I find it hard to believe that I am special enough for someone to care for and like, for someone to make love to in a gentle fashion, for someone to want to get to know who I am. I have approached every single relationship I have ever had with those beliefs. I have had relationships with people who have beaten me, raped me, or refused to talk to me, touch me or be friendly to me. I have had relationships with people whose names I struggled to remember, or who I didn't really like, know or trust. I have given up my freedom and let myself be controlled because I was so desperate for safety. I thought I could exchange myself in order to feel safe.

I married someone who used walls of silence and ill temper to keep me at arm's length. I found it unbearable not knowing what I had done to displease him, or how to make it right. Everything I tried seemed to make his distaste for me worse. I craved physical contact and emotional closeness, and ended up angry and resentful, as well as isolated and anxious. I felt there must be something very wrong with me if my husband didn't want me. I didn't know that I was a beautiful child of God who deserves love.

Since my marriage ended a bit less than two years ago I have been on a real journey. I have stayed single, not because I really want to, but because I feel like I have a precious opportunity to do it right, or at least better, than the first time around. I have been in recovery for over nine years, but I have never been single in recovery until now. It is horribly painful, but I feel like I have a chance for a new life, because I have a toolkit to help me to build one.

I have begun to discover that my lack of understanding about intimacy underpins pretty much my whole disease. If I could reduce all my problems down to one phrase it would be, "I do not know what intimacy is." I don't know who I am. I don't know what love is. I cannot form relationships with other people because I have nothing authentic to offer them. I don't know how to let go of my fear enough to be able to sit with myself or anyone else and form real closeness.

The only way I can see to address this is to open my heart to my Higher Power. I have enough trust in the program and feel safe enough in the process to take a chance on surrendering what I don't know. I have finally put my trust in a Sponsor. I read from Conference Approved Literature every day. I get to as many meetings as I can. I share when I can. I do service when I can. I get involved, I connect, I surrender. It isn't rocket science. Like I have heard, it's a simple program for complicated people, and that's how it is for me. I work the Steps and the Traditions, I follow the guidelines and try and learn how to communicate and behave in a healthy way—one that is a better reflection of my Higher Power's love for me than my will. It's funny but the more I let go, the more I find myself. The more I open myself to the possibility that I am lovable, the less I seem to crave attention. I feel like there is a real possibility for a relationship built upon intimacy in the future, but I have a lot of work to do to get there.

In the meantime, I count my blessings. I used to dream of being a part of a community and being with people who I could be open with, and I have that now! In some ways I have already realized my dreams, but now I have to dare myself to dream even more wildly. I believe I can have a life that is connected, peaceful, stable, safe and full of love. Maybe one day I will know what intimately sharing myself with another person is really like. I am so fortunate to have the safety I always wanted, the company I always craved and the depth of connection I always dreamed I would have.

Al-Anon gave me the tools to learn intimacy

In the two years that led up to my partner's first day of sobriety, he spiraled out of control, and so did I. We were equals in sacrificing one another's well-being. We both arranged nights with multiple sex partners, complete with drugs and plenty of alcohol. At that point neither of us was capable of any intimacy with one another, looking instead for a connection outside of our relationship. I knew that I couldn't control his desire to drink, but I could manipulate him into bringing other partners

19

home, allowing me to attempt to get the emotional attention I desperately craved from another source.

When he became sober, we abandoned this lifestyle with great relief. Our sex life was better than ever for the first few weeks, but it didn't last. One of the consequences of our promiscuity was that my partner became HIV-positive—as if we needed another block to reclaiming intimacy! But I was to discover that sex is only one small part of intimacy, and my reactive nature proved to be a sizeable stumbling block in my recovery.

I grew up in a family where drinking was either completely forbidden by some or liberally enjoyed by others. This dichotomy made me understand early on that alcohol was something special, something that signaled rebellion, and the folks who drank it were utterly free. But the reality of the behavior it caused quickly poisoned that image. I was deeply affected by others' drinking, especially that of the men in my immediate family.

In my family, it was normal for me to be physically close to female relatives, but not with male relatives, and even less with those who were drinking. Being close with my father and step-father was particularly challenging as a gay child, who often felt so decidedly different from everyone else. As an adult, I had no framework to reference when it came to expressing intimacy. I remember feeling lost and creating a protective wall between myself and my partner. I was always reserved, not heeding my own call to generosity or accepting the well-intentioned physical generosity of my caring partner.

In recovery, I've learned that generating intimacy involves using a lot of the tools I've acquired in Al-Anon. First and foremost, I keep the focus on myself, developing a compassionate understanding and an unconditional forgiveness of my past behavior. I did the best with what I had, but now I have something better. Second, it means that I always tell my partner what I want, and he tells me what he wants. I don't expect for him to know how I'm feeling, and I don't expect to know how he's feeling unless there's a real and honest dialogue between the two of us. Third, I keep aware at all times of my tendency to isolate. When I feel like I'm ready to withdraw for whatever reason, real or perceived, I know that it's time to open up and bring that impulse into the light of recovery.

Intimacy isn't just something involving my partner. It is an open and vulnerable way of doing things in life that can be cultivated in all my relationships by full listening, being present in the moment as it happens (not as I wish it were happening) and keeping my reactive and judgmental past in check. It means being ready to admit that I was wrong, and it means being ready to do things differently.

I found a way to rely on myself instead of others

Growing up in a family affected by alcoholism, I learned to seek emotional and spiritual support outside of myself. I looked to others to know what I should be thinking, how I should be feeling and how to mimic a "relationship with God." I listened to others' opinions to determine my self-worth and to gauge whether I was okay. I frequently compared myself to other people, or to an imaginary model of perfection, to see how I measured up.

I looked to others to confirm that I was physically attractive. I thought that if I could get someone to like me, it would mean that I was worthy of love. Once I had captured that person's heart, however, I had no idea what to do with it! I didn't know what it meant to share myself with another person, because I didn't even know who I was without the other person as a reference point.

Now I know that with the help of Al-Anon principles, including the Seventh Tradition ("Every group ought to be fully self-supporting, declining outside contributions."), I can be fully self-supporting. I don't have to look to my friends or intimate partner to know that I am worthy of love.

Instead, I can look to myself and to my Higher Power. I also have a relationship with my Higher Power and a spiritual connection to other people that is grounded within myself rather than modeled after what other people have told me is the "right" way to relate to God. I can offer love and support to others without giving up who I am, because I have the tools to provide myself with emotional and spiritual support.

Being fully self-supporting doesn't mean I never rely on others. It does mean that when I want or need something from my partner, I can ask for it. It also means that I am okay, regardless of whether he is able to provide it.

Sex didn't fill the need for intimacy

I never understood why nearly every boy I had slept with could just toss me aside, but when I went to my first Al-Anon adult children meeting, I read about the common character traits of those who grew up with alcoholism. Something beautiful happened when I read that adult children of alcoholics often confuse sex with intimacy.

Immediately, tears began to stream down my face as my past suddenly made sense. The only way I knew to get close to anyone was physically. I was desperate for intimacy, but all I got was sex. This was when Al-Anon helped me to start changing my attitude—and therefore my life—for the better. My pattern of promiscuity suddenly made sense, and the guilt I carried was released. I promised myself that I would never again abuse my body and let others take advantage of my vulnerability. I started learning how to respect myself, regaining the self-confidence that I had lost through years of promiscuity.

I felt safe holding my father's hand

It is unfortunate that the word intimacy has, in popular usage, become a euphemism for a sexual relationship. In all the Al-Anon meetings I've attended where the topic has come up, the sharing tends to gravitate towards sex. For me, however, an equally compelling side of the subject is emotional intimacy which, in my case, has nothing to do with sex.

I grew up in a household where intimacy did not stand much of a chance. My father worked an evening shift; we did not see him except on weekends. He was a taciturn man, approachable but not accessible. My mother was a woman who did not display emotion. Although she loved her children, she did not show her affection very readily. Her idea of touching her kids constituted an occasional flick of her finger to my head. My sister recalls that she never sat on our mother's lap.

My parents were good people, but they were clueless when it came to emotional intimacy. Despite this chilly environment, I was not totally frozen out. I learned the meaning of emotional intimacy inadvertently from my father, as I shall relate.

On Saturday mornings, when I was about six years old, my father and I would walk to the butcher shop about eight blocks from home. Ever-silent, he would take my hand in his. Now my father had the largest hands imaginable to a six-year-old boy, owing probably to nature and to his work. When my small hand was swallowed up in his, I had an indescribable feeling of joy, of intimacy. I felt that as long as he held my hand, I was as safe as anyone could possibly be. I felt that there was nothing in the world to fear as long as my hand was held in his. What I think I experienced was emotional intimacy of the highest order.

Unfortunately, when we returned from the butcher shop, and my hand was no longer in his, I fell back into my everyday pattern of being emotionally on my own. Ironically, I experienced the heights to which emotional intimacy could rise from the very person who, for the most part, ignored me. Yet my minimal experience was enough to make me vow to be emotionally close to my own children when I became a father. Life being what it is, however, I retained enough of my father's standoffishness that my attempts at emotional intimacy with my children have taken considerable time to improve.

I learned intimacy by working the Steps with my Sponsor

Growing up in the disease of alcoholism, my focus was always outside of myself. Coming into the program as an adult, I knew very little about the person I spent the most time with—me. In fact, coming to meetings was the first time I had ever made a commitment to my own well-being. Supported by the fellowship, I was encouraged to develop relationships with myself and a Higher Power as well as other human beings.

The process of working the Steps with a Sponsor is an excellent way to learn about intimate relationships. My favorite shorthand expression for learning to trust is "came to believe." In the same way that Step Two ("Came to believe that a Power greater than ourselves could restore us to sanity") encouraged me to gradually understand a Power greater than myself, I found I could apply this wisdom to relationships with others and myself.

The more I learned about and came to accept myself through the Steps, the more I trusted my Higher Power and became willing to share myself more intimately with others. This has had profound effects on all my relationships. I am even more willing to share what is appropriate with the active alcoholic.

Knowing I can share all my secrets with at least one other human being and my Higher Power makes me more willing to take risks outside of Al-Anon and with my family.

I should be intimate with myself first

Someday, I want to be married and be in an intimate relationship with the man I will marry. I know I can do neither without using the Al-Anon tools in my life.

How can I be intimate with another person unless I am intimate with myself? How can I share with another person before I share me with me? This is where Step Four ("Made a searching and fearless moral inventory of ourselves") and Step Five ("Admitted to God, to ourselves, and to another human being the exact nature of our wrongs") come in.

After completing an excruciating Fourth Step, I began my Fifth Step a few months ago. I have done Fourth Steps before, but never at this gut level. I am cleaning out the core. I am looking inside me. I am bravely standing and facing my strengths and my struggles. First peeking, I am now looking and finally seeing into myself. Tempted to run, I choose to stay. I choose to keep coming back to me.

Questions for Reflection

1. How do I feel when I hear the word "intimacy"? When I think about being intimate with someone, what is my response?

2. In which relationships do I expect to have a level of intimacy? How close do I feel to the people with whom I share this type of relationship?

3. What am I looking for in intimate relationships? Which relationships in my life display some of these qualities?

4. What do I know about myself? How is this different from what I know about others?

5. In what ways am I willing to share my inner thoughts and feelings with another person? In what ways am I willing to admit these things to myself?

6. How close do I feel to the people in my life? What barriers prevent me from feeling as close to others as I would like?

7. To which people in my life do I want to feel closer? In what ways have I attempted to be more intimate with others? What has been the result?

8. What changes have I seen in my relationships since coming into Al-Anon? How have they affected my feelings towards others? Towards myself?

Chapter Two

Building and Rebuilding Trust

For those of us who have lived with the disease of alcoholism, the idea of being open and honest in a loving way may seem like an impossible dream. In the alcoholic situation, we often came to doubt ourselves and mistrust those around us. Overwhelmed by fear, we may have lost the ability to speak up for ourselves. We may have tried to please the alcoholic or others in our lives to the point that we have forgotten what pleases us. After hiding our true selves for so long, we may not even remember who we really are. The less we reveal of ourselves to the people we love, the less we are able to fully participate in those relationships.

In Al-Anon, we gradually learn how to trust ourselves again, to value ourselves and to have confidence in our worth as human beings. Working the Twelve Steps brings us awareness of the part we have played in our relationships, and we get the chance to make amends. It is important to remember that, although we may want to have a more intimate relationship with the alcoholic or others in our lives, we cannot force another person to be close to us. If we want to experience intimacy, the only place we can start is with ourselves.

Here are some members' experiences in building trust:

- "Sometimes I struggle to find balance between taking care of myself and trusting."

- "I refrain from opening my own detective agency or questioning to the nth degree."

- "I had to learn how to take care of myself outside the bedroom before I could trust myself in the bedroom."

- "Just as the saying goes 'we can't truly love someone else until we love ourselves,' perhaps we can't truly be intimate with another until we have been truly intimate with ourselves."

- "Emotional intimacy had slipped away, until I no longer had the trust that my husband even cared about me."

- "I came to realize that the emotional and physical intimacy that was lacking in my alcoholic marriage was a direct result of lack of trust and the inability to build a strong foundation in our relationship."

- "I can only get what I give. How can I expect the alcoholic to be loving or intimate with me if I am not that way with him? Now that he is in recovery, I need to remember that this is a different man with new possibilities and that I am a new woman in recovery, too."

- "I started to believe I was worthy of experiencing physical as well as emotional joy. Allowing myself to feel meant I had to trust my husband. Trust did not come easy."

- "I trust no one completely. I've always got one eye looking over my shoulder."

As we learn to trust and appreciate ourselves, we can open up to others, creating room in our lives for them, allowing them the opportunity to be in relationship with us, if they choose. With the help of Al-Anon, we can find healthy ways to connect with others in our lives, allowing us to reach out to them while still taking care of ourselves.

Members Share Experience, Strength and Hope

It was hard to let people see the real me

As a young woman, I believed intimacy was getting naked with the opposite sex. Years later, I attended an Al-Anon workshop and found a new meaning for intimacy: actually trusting another human being enough to reveal my true self. Wow! That was something I was not prepared to do. I think growing up with an alcoholic parent destroyed my trust in others. Survival depended on never letting anyone know the real me.

I was living with a man I loved for about eight years. Sexual intimacy was easy, but he knew only what I let him see of my emotions and feelings. Mostly he saw me being what I thought the situation required. I recall the feeling that I was always wearing a mask, playing a role.

In time I came to reveal some of my true self to my Sponsor and other close friends from Al-Anon and A.A.: Always other women, never men. It was a slow process, as I would let some of me "out" and wait for the rejection. It never came! What a wonderful feeling. I could be accepted and even loved, in spite of my flaws.

Eventually my lover and I came to trust each other enough to marry. Slowly we each revealed more of ourselves. Then I found that I had cancer. This was a terrible blow. However, it forced me to accept assistance from my husband. I came to trust him enough to be fully intimate in our relationship.

I thought I was through with intimacy

Opening up and letting anyone in on a personal level has been a real process for me. Intimacy scares me even at this age. I am 73, and I am scared to death to let you see what is inside me because I know you won't like me anymore. Even though I am afraid of it, I know that is what I want today in my relationships.

The first intimacy I ever received was 21 years ago when I began going to Al-Anon. I began to open up and share my pain. The shell began to crack.

My father sexually abused me as a child, so I felt unsafe in my home. I never told my mother or anyone else until I got into Al-Anon. I pretty much shut down all my feelings at that point except fear. I hated the small town where I grew up, as everybody always knew everybody's business. The message I got was, "Don't talk, don't trust and don't feel. You definitely don't tell anyone else what's going on in your home. What happens here, stays here. When you walk out this door you put on a happy face." I often heard, "If you don't stop crying, I will give you something to cry about." I stopped crying in front of everyone at that point. I was not about to let anyone know what I was thinking or feeling. So that left me with not a clue what real intimacy or trust was all about.

Then I met Mr. Wonderful, who introduced me to alcoholism. The intimacy was only about sex and more confusion. I did get four wonderful children out of that marriage. The marriage didn't last but the children did. I was alone raising my children for 11 years before I met another nice man who was also an alcoholic, because I did nothing to change me. That marriage ended in my husband's death but resulted in me getting into Al-Anon and staying. The third marriage was more of a dry drunk situation and didn't work either. I will be eternally grateful to Al-Anon for giving me the tools of working the Steps to survive getting out of that relationship.

By now, I figured I had experienced enough intimacy to last me for a lifetime, when at 72, I met a really special person, who treats me like a queen. I am very reluctantly learning to trust love one more time, "One Day at a Time." The key for me is opening up—saying my truth, my feelings, my opinions. I'm letting others have their truth, their feelings and their opinions, while I agree to disagree and "Live and Let Live."

For me, sponsorship has helped me to love, to trust, to feel—to love myself no matter what. I never intended to be married this many times and for years I carried a lot of guilt and shame about my past. Thanks to many Fourth Step inventories, I know it just is what it is. I know today that in truly forgiving myself, I accept that the past can't be any different.

I believe my Higher Power has a plan for my life and I am not in charge. I thank Al-Anon every day for the love and friends I have received through being in this wonderful program. The miracle of finally being able to open up and trust others is the true intimacy I have always searched for and found in the rooms of recovery. I know I will continue to go to meetings for the rest of my life.

I built a protective wall around myself

One thing that has become very evident to me in my journey of working my Al-Anon program is how much the family disease of alcoholism affected my husband and me, our marriage, and our children. We both grew up in homes where alcohol was an issue. I believe because of that, the relationship tools we brought to the marriage included lack of respect, manipulation, unhealthy communication and a lack of common courtesy. Needless to say, over the years this developed into resentment, anger, hurt, fear, sarcastic comments and being judgmental, on both our parts. His progressing alcoholism over the years only added fuel to the fire.

Not feeling I could trust the person who was supposed to be my greatest support was heart-wrenching, and affected so many parts of my life. It took away the closeness I wanted us to have. I wanted someone who was supportive, someone who listened, someone I could share things with and someone to be close to physically. Instead, alcoholism gave me a wonderful man with so much hurt and pain that the only way he could find to survive was through drinking and lashing out at those closest to him with harsh words and lies.

My husband has now been sober for a couple of years and we have been focusing on rebuilding our relationship. All of the dishonesty, lying and manipulation that goes with the disease took a huge toll on us, especially my issues of trust. As a result, over the years, I'd built this great big wall around me as a means of protection, so I wouldn't get hurt. I see now that this didn't protect me; it merely isolated me and kept me focused on my pain.

Today, by attending meetings, sharing with my Sponsor and working the Twelve Steps, I've arrived at a place where I want to dismantle that wall and start to take it down. One part of me is fearful because I know that by doing so, it leaves me open to the chance of being hurt again. But I also know that if I don't take that chance, I will never move forward, learn to trust again or rebuild this relationship with my husband, who is a sensitive and caring man. It takes a real trust in my Higher Power to have the faith to open myself up to the chance of being hurt. But I do know that taking that leap of faith can give me the chance for a relationship based on trust, mutual respect and consideration—true intimacy, the relationship I believe my Higher Power wants us to have.

My possessiveness came out of fear

When I learned that my wife had an affair I was devastated— not because I hadn't done the same, but because it meant that there was a possibility that she would leave me. Up until this point in my life, I was not capable of intimacy because the fear of abandonment influenced most of my decisions in my primary relationships. Unconsciously, I had picked someone who I thought would never leave me because she was sick, less than me, did not believe in divorce and had frequent sex with me. This seemed to be the perfect formula based on my observations of my alcoholic mother.

They say that gifts come in a funny box, and that Al-Anon can transform our losses. Well, my wife's affair was that gift! It was what I needed to face my fear of abandonment. The pain of not changing had become greater than the fear of changing. My loving Sponsor at the time asked me a very important question: "What is it about you that makes you fit with someone who has an affair?" The answer was that I thought I wasn't lovable, so I objectified people, especially women, so that they would add some value to me. Only a person who thought he or she was an object would allow this, hence the affair.

Facing the fear of abandonment and the realization that I objectified women allowed me to release my belief of "ownership" of the person. This freedom gave me the space I needed to start my healing and journey of discovering who I really am, and that I am lovable just the way I am. As my self-love grew, my love for others also grew and I eventually met my current mate. She has helped me redefine intimacy. We share with each other our most vulnerable thoughts, feelings and experiences. We are individuals, and self-supporting by our own contributions. Our sexual relationship is an outward expression of an inner connection. The only thing that my relationship in recovery has in common with my relationship in the disease is its purpose for me to grow closer to my Higher Power.

I needed inner growth to handle the outside world

My relationship with myself was so damaged by years of abuse from my parents and brothers that I was unkind to myself. I have been locked away inside myself most of my life, unable to form close relationships with anyone. There was too much stuff to hide, too much shame.

The first step was to heal the damage enough to feel something positive about myself. Integral to this process was believing that there was an "other" who also felt positively about me. This was a Higher Power who valued me and cared about me. I was encouraged to form a relationship with a Higher Power of my choosing. I chose a Higher Power who was supportive instead of critical, kind instead of mean and loving instead of threatening. This was a protracted process of coming to believe. At first, I could dream and wish that there would be a Higher Power who wished me well, but I couldn't really believe it was true. Gradually the voices telling me of my lack of worth, my stupidity, and that no one would ever like me were interrupted (every once in a while) by a voice that said, "good job," "you're doing the best you can" or "be kind to yourself."

Getting to know myself, take care of myself and trust myself was, I believe, how I formed an intimate relationship with myself. Only then was I ready to start learning how to take this new self out into the company of others. Only when I felt I didn't have to defend myself against my inside world could I reveal myself to my outside world. Al-Anon was the place where I could first try this out, a little safe place to experiment. This outside world was not critical, was not mean, did not gossip about me. Instead, it reflected back to me a positive image—I was as worthy as anyone, I could be heard like anyone and I could give to and receive from all. I developed trust for others.

Then, I was ready to take myself into the world outside of Al-Anon. I knew what good and kind people looked like, and just had to look for them and, a little bit at a time, get to know them while letting them get to know me. I had better radar for detecting who was not going to respect my emerging self and who did not deserve my trust. I developed a thicker skin and knew that someone else behaving badly toward me was not a reflection of me. The boundary was clearer between who I was and who they were. I could remain okay no matter what someone else thought of me.

My forays into relationships with others—into being who I am with others and liking who I am with others—are works in progress. I am still afraid of forming an intimate relationship with a partner. I guess that is my current step. It involves letting down a final set of defenses and fears. But I just go one step at a time and believe that if this happens it will be part of the process and the time will be right. If it doesn't happen, I can enjoy the other newfound relationships that keep coming my way. I can trust my Higher Power even more and believe that the process is happening on time and as needed.

Trust is not just blind faith

I always considered myself a very trusting person, willing to be completely open and vulnerable. I thought this was one of my biggest character assets. Taking a personal inventory and sharing it with another person (Steps Four and Five) showed me that I trusted with a blind naiveté that was more denial than trust. When that denial was shattered in my marriage to an alcoholic, I swung to the other side of the pendulum (as usual) and felt like I could never trust my wife again.

Continually taking my own inventory has helped me find a healthy middle ground. I can choose to be vulnerable while keeping my eyes open to reality. It was a long and difficult journey back to opening myself up again. I've found that trust, like love, is sometimes a decision rather than a feeling. Today, if I choose to be in an intimate relationship with someone, I choose to be open, honest and trusting. If someone I love proves themselves unworthy of this intimacy, I can choose to accept that reality and take steps to do what is best for me.

I have to feel safe enough to trust

For most of my life, I have lived in an environment that was hostile and constantly changing for the worse. I learned to not want anything or to cherish anything lest it be used against me and as a means to torment me. I could trust only one person, my father, and yet he was unable to be there for me when his work took him out of town. When he was home, he was not a demonstrative person. He had been taken from our native culture and raised in the residential schools, then left home at 14, so he had no tools to teach me how to be close and open with another person. My brothers were much older than me and rarely had any time to concern themselves with someone so much younger than they were. There was much laughter in our home, but it was only on the surface. It was like we all wore clown makeup when people were watching, then took off the masks behind closed doors. Almost all of the people who should have cared for me and nourished my soul were instead afflicted by this disease and had only pain and shame to share with anyone.

So, having grown up in this world, I had no concept of what a loving relationship should look like. When I started to date, I would mistake someone being okay with me being around for genuine affection. Then if someone showed some affection for me, I would mistake it for genuine intimacy. For myself, I had no idea who I was or what I wanted and no clear path to finding myself—I was a lost soul, as so many of us are in this disease. So for me, today, after having worked the Steps a number of times, I find that I can be quite affectionate with a person, but if I know nothing about them, or if they do not know themselves and what they want, then it is not possible to be intimate. To be intimate with a person, I must be able to—first of all—identify my own fears, wants, needs and passions. Then, once I have identified those things, I must feel safe enough to share them with someone else. If I don't feel safe enough to open myself up, at least partly at first, then I can never attain a level of intimacy that we all deserve to experience. A person can have deep affection for another and know how they will respond in a given situation, but true intimacy is knowing the history behind that response and why they will take that action.

In order for me to feel truly intimate with someone, I must be able to tell them my worst fears, obsessions and compulsions, and feel safe that they will never use it against me. With time in recovery, I have removed most of the buttons—actually wounds that never healed properly—that are very sensitive, and I can now share most of my bad stuff and yet remain unaffected if someone thinks that this somehow gives them power over me or a weapon to use against me. I have enough faith in my Higher Power that, whatever other people say to me today, I can put it into context: Either they are spiritually fit and I should listen, or they are spiritually sick and are trying to share their pain so that it might be somehow lessened.

To be affectionate to another person is to enjoy being around them; to be intimate with another person is to know why you like them. I cannot consider myself to be in a truly intimate relationship with another person if I find myself unable to tell them something. I know today that I can tell my wife anything, anywhere, at any time, and she will accept it and not think less of me. I have shared all of my deepest, darkest secrets with her and she has never said that I was "less than" for having those thoughts or experiences. Of course, this doesn't mean that I always tell her everything. I am, after all, a product of my environment, and my first instinct, in pretty much any situation, is to cover up and manipulate the situation. But with the help of my Higher Power and my relationship with my Sponsor, I am getting past that.

I had to choose between being vulnerable and keeping my secret

When I read the phrase "sexual abuse" aloud in *From Survival to Recovery* (B-21), I smiled to myself. Even though two years in Al-Anon had given me safety, I'd already decided that some life experiences would go to the grave with me! Sexual abuse was one. I even felt contempt when others shared about childhood sexual abuse. But now I wondered if God was trying to get me to face it, to admit it out loud.

I had a decision to make: I could choose not to comment on the reading, not share my personal experience, keep my life to myself and leave with my secret intact—or I could be vulnerable, invite others to intimately know me, put the shame on the rightful owner and allow God into my trauma. In recovery, I'd gotten a tiny, inviting taste of the self-love that comes from being genuine, and, in that moment, I wanted it more than I wanted to protect myself. I chose to say quietly: "Yes, I relate." I had no idea how I had helped myself with those words. The next time I read "sexual abuse" aloud in a subsequent meeting, tears rolled down my cheeks. I had begun to grieve, to feel.

This time I decided to "act as if"

In my family of origin, showing love was seen as a sign of weakness and could be used against you. From the outside we looked like a family that liked to hug, but from the inside, those hugs came at a price. Judgment and criticism were the norm. I might feel loved in one moment and, in the next, shamed and criticized for having emotional needs. It was a dangerous place to be full of fear.

A few months ago I was on vacation with my family, the one I created as an adult. In the past if my husband tried to get close and put an arm around me, I would pull away, saying I needed my space. This time I decided to "act as if" and instead of pulling away, I leaned into him. I allowed myself to show him that I love him, need him and want him. It felt right. It was a moment of serenity on vacation on a beautiful beach.

Later that night, he thanked me for not pulling away. I was touched that he not only noticed but said something in a way I could hear it. I am not being attacked anymore. There is nothing to fear. I allowed myself to experience some serenity. My recovery allows me to "act as if."

Taking an intimacy inventory helps me know when to trust

Early on in my recovery, an Al-Anon friend shared with me four simple questions to ask myself in gauging the safety of my relationships. These have stayed with me through the years and have helped me immensely in learning to trust—one of the very necessary ingredients of intimacy. They are as follows:

1. Are there at least a couple things you really like about each other?

2. Do you share a similar sense of ethics?

3. Do you encourage each other to move forward, or hold each other back?

4. How do you each treat the people who no longer matter to you, because someday you might not matter to each other?

These questions give me a frame of reference—something I never had in growing up with others equally affected by the family disease of alcoholism. I ask them of myself periodically in each of the variety of relationships I have. The answers often change as the relationships progress, sometimes in one direction, and sometimes in another. I've learned that my answers don't necessarily indicate a course of action, like "Stay away from this person," or "This one's a keeper." They just help me take the temperature and be aware.

If my answers do change regarding a relationship, it reminds me to adjust my actions—and my trust level—accordingly. Prior to Al-Anon, I didn't always give myself the freedom to change my mind. Once I made a decision, I felt stuck with it. By asking myself these questions, I've felt more comfortable putting more distance between some people and getting closer to others—even those who at one time I held at bay.

Relationships can change, and it's important for me to be aware of that. When I am, I can make reasonable decisions based on current circumstances as well as feelings.

I am gradually earning my spouse's trust again

When I came into Al-Anon, I had no idea how much healing and recovery would take place—or even that I needed it. I just knew I had to get relief from somewhere. Insanity had a tight hold on me and I was spinning out of control. I had grown up in an alcoholic home and had unknowingly married into one as well.

I always tried to keep up with the drinkers, while silently scorning their actions. I detested alcoholics and was determined to punish my husband with my own actions. My alcoholic spouse of more than 20 years had previously had at least one affair that I knew of, so I started cheating on him. I was fully leading a double life, actively dating and lying to everyone. I told my prospects that I wore a wedding ring to "ward off weirdos." I was telling so many twisted stories that I couldn't keep up. I was experiencing so much insanity, and my coping mechanisms were failing me.

It all caught up with me, and I almost lost all that I truly treasure. The program saved me from myself, from my corrosive resentments and self-destruction. Four years after hitting rock bottom, I am still learning what intimacy is. Intimacy is about being authentic in my own life and honest with myself. When I stop covering up for myself and alcoholics, I become free.

I have had a long, hard road, and have stayed in my marriage. The trust between us was wrecked, and it has taken years to gain back even a portion of what I once had. I feel a different and deeper connection to my spouse now. I am grateful for him in a way I never felt before. It helps me not to dwell on the past. I feel better about everything today, and I know all I have is this day.

My Sponsor has helped me the most with intimacy. She does not judge me, but guides me gently through the Steps and my important Fourth Step work. In my relationship with my Sponsor, I am learning the meaning of intimacy by experiencing it and working to not be so closed off. I have never trusted anyone with my true self, thoughts and emotions. I have had so much disappointment and hurt throughout the years that vulnerability is a scary prospect, but I no longer want to be false or blocked by trying to protect myself. Those walls never saved me anyway.

This is my challenge and my aim: To be free of my many tall walls, and to build bridges where I can. I experience healing and faith through this process, and I don't walk alone.

I couldn't afford to show weakness

I grew up with alcoholism in my family and identify with Al-Anon as an adult child. It wasn't until I began Al-Anon that I discovered I did not know how to be intimate in any relationship. I could not identify my feelings and when I finally did find emotions, I was terrified to share them with anyone. I recognized I kept a safe distance in all my relationships—with friends, coworkers and family alike. I had hidden behind a facade of perfectionism and could not admit any type of weakness. Being emotional equated to being weak!

I began to realize my relationship with my husband lacked intimacy. I had married a man who, for different reasons than mine, was not able to express himself emotionally. As I began to attend meetings, read literature and perform small acts of service, I was able to test the waters of sharing bits of myself. I started with my group, and from there, let myself show some of my weaknesses to my friends. I have since discovered this word "weakness" should be taken out of my personal vocabulary. I am not weak, I am human. Understanding I was a human being, made by my Higher Power, helped relieve some of the shame I felt and encouraged me to further explore my emotional and spiritual self. When I shared personal vulnerabilities, the people in my life responded. They identified with me. Feelings of intimacy began to sprout, and the more chances I took, the bigger and better my relationships got. My marital relationship changed as I reacted differently to my spouse. There were fewer arguments because my need to be right was decreasing and my need to be in a caring, honest, emotional partnership was growing.

I have journeyed so far in Al-Anon. I am a complicated being and this self-discovery will continue for a lifetime. The little girl who felt so alone, afraid, ashamed and wore a mask of happiness is growing up. I still have work to do. While I asked someone to be my Sponsor, I have not been able to fully open myself to this relationship. I still feel vulnerable—too vulnerable to fully open myself to any one person. The joyous thing is I can be myself with my Higher Power. What a gift! I know I will continue to grow in my journey of intimacy through the Al-Anon program.

Questions for Reflection

1. How well do I know myself? What kind of person do I consider myself to be?

2. Under what circumstances do I behave in a trustworthy fashion? In what situations do I find it difficult to be trustworthy?

3. How well do I keep promises to other people? How well do I keep promises to myself?

4. How have I betrayed another's trust? What can I do to start to rebuild that trust?

5. What prevents me from trusting others? From trusting myself?

6. How do I decide who is deserving of my trust? Which Al-Anon tools can help me determine whom to trust?

7. How do I behave around untrustworthy people? Which Al-Anon principles can I use to navigate a betrayal of trust?

8. How do I feel about revealing my true self to someone else? What might keep me from being open with another person?

9. Is there anyone I'm willing to trust enough to be truly open? What qualities do they have that inspire trust in me?

Chapter Three

Communicating Clearly

When we walk into the rooms of Al-Anon, many of us are shocked at how openly and honestly other members share in meetings. In the alcoholic situation, this kind of directness was often completely unheard of. We were much more used to hiding or masking our own thoughts and feelings or bottling them up until we exploded. The others in our lives, too, likely had no better communication skills than we did.

Sharing our thoughts and feelings with the alcoholic or others in our lives often resulted in being ridiculed, degraded or simply ignored. Faced with such treatment, many of us shut down any impulse to share what was genuine about ourselves with those we love—much less anyone else. Others among us became compulsive truth-tellers, attempting to unburden ourselves on the nearest person, whether they were willing to listen or not. Unfortunately, neither of these reactions actually helped us feel more accepted or loved.

Numerous members have shared their experiences on the subject of communication:

- "It was heartbreaking to see the way alcoholism stripped away the person I loved dearly, until there seemed no vestige of communication between us that wasn't steeped in denial or misunderstanding. I came to see how I was suffering bereavement, even though no one had actually died."

- "When I was having difficulty with our teenage daughter, my husband and I ended up in counseling. and our assignment was to share feelings with one another. I used to be the one initiating the conversation and became tired of doing it, so we stopped sharing."

- "Neither one of us knew how to be emotionally honest and neither one of us knew how to problem-solve or negotiate differences. Consequently, our relationship deteriorated into a lot of bullying, yelling, passive-aggressive behavior, martyrdom, blaming and shaming."

- "Thinking back, it amazes me how often and loudly my parents, three siblings and I talked without ever really saying anything, especially about our feelings."

- "My vision of a family gathered around a roaring fire sipping spiked cider and laughing does not match up with reality. My family has no skills at conversing or laughing together because we have no sober experiences doing it."

- "I honestly thought my husband should know what I want without my having to tell him, and I have no doubt that I probably punished him for his failure to read my mind."

- "I didn't learn how to share in a conversation, just to answer the questions of others in a general way or to relate some incident that didn't reveal too much about me."

- "Intimate and sexual relations were subject to the power and control games and emotional and mental abuse cycle. While I might have tried to be consistent by asserting my needs and desires, this communication would be regularly disregarded or neglected by my partner, reinforcing my sense of lack of control and lower self-esteem."

- "For many years I have craved emotional intimacy with my father, a sober alcoholic. But his desire to be right all the time, his need for me to agree with him and his anger when I don't, prevent me from ever sharing myself with him."

- "I went into every relationship feeling like I had to interpret what the other person wanted, and deliver it whether I felt right about it or not. I ended up angry and rageful because I had no way to get my needs met. In fact, I couldn't even identify my needs."

- "Although I was always a good listener in relationships and was a trustworthy friend to others, I rarely felt comfortable sharing much about myself. I felt secretly unworthy and ashamed of how much anger and neediness I carried inside."

- "I grew up in 'Happy Valley,' where happiness was the only acceptable emotion expressed in my family. I learned to stuff my feelings and show with my poker face that I was happy on the outside, no matter what was happening on the inside."

- "My life was marked by poor communication—subtle hints, veiled threats, all-out crazy rants or hurtful silence."

- "As his alcoholism progressed and my reaction to it intensified, I came to realize that sex had been a way to mask our inability to communicate with each other. We had make-up sex after arguments instead of talking about what happened and trying to resolve it."

One of the core principles of the Al-Anon program is rigorous self-honesty. If we aren't dealing honestly with ourselves, we cannot deal with reality as it is. Hiding from the truth in denial and fear will only leave us trapped in an impossible situation. It is only through recognizing and acknowledging the truth that we become capable of making healthy decisions for ourselves.

Step Five can serve as a guide through the process of learning how to be honest: with ourselves, our Higher Power, and another human being. Admitting our character defects—and assets—is admitting the truth about ourselves. Once we can look at our lives as they really are, we become gradually more able to communicate that truth with others.

Gaining the courage to speak openly and honestly about ourselves is only half of what makes good communication. The other half is learning how to listen. The fear of judgment and shame that kept so many of us from sharing our authentic selves also kept us on our guard, readying our defenses for the next inevitable attack. If we are busy thinking about what we are going to say next, we are not listening.

Al-Anon meetings were perhaps the first place we learned what it meant to really listen. By practicing in meetings, we became able to let our thoughts rest while someone else was talking, so that we could really hear what they were saying. Eventually, the practice of listening in meetings spread to other areas of our lives, as we learned to "practice these principles in all our affairs" (Step Twelve).

But what happens when the people in our lives—alcoholics or otherwise—are unwilling or unable to communicate clearly with us? What then? No matter how much we may wish to, we cannot control whether or not another person is able to share honestly with us or listen to us. Communication is a two-way street, but we are only responsible for our side. If we are unable to have a face-to-face conversation, perhaps we could express our feelings some other way. Writing a letter or sending an email or text message may be a more effective method of speaking our piece while letting go of the results.

Unfortunately, there is no guarantee that the people in our lives will respond positively to our efforts. Sharing our thoughts with a Sponsor or other trusted friend can also provide some relief. Whether or not it is reciprocated, doing our part to communicate clearly can give us a clearer understanding of ourselves and our needs. This, in turn, will give us a firmer foundation upon which to build our relationships—with others as well as ourselves.

Members Share Experience, Strength and Hope

Communicating my feelings prevents resentments

I have been married for 35 years to a wonderful woman. We both come from alcoholic homes and had never dealt with the issues associated with that. Speaking for my own part, I was a caretaker, both professionally and in my personal life as well. I had to guess at what my feelings were or should be, or what a normal person would have done in a certain situation.

I loved my wife the best that I could, but I had no self-love. I was never really sure what the word "love" meant. It had no meaningful use in my family of origin. Yet my wife and I had a reasonably satisfying sexual life for these many years. I believe that I got my basic needs met.

My wife and I are in recovery now. My wife has been in for two-and-a-half years and I have been in for three months. Since I have joined her in recovery, there have been many changes in our emotional intimacy and therefore our sexual intimacy.

I began to come out with my resentments. At first, I was angry and accusatory. I quickly saw them for what they were: My "stuff," literally and figuratively speaking. I had "stuffed" these feelings for 30 years for "wrongs" done to me, so of course they were my issues. A healthy person would have brought them up at the time and dealt with them.

The last big resentment had to do with poor communication about and during sex. It was a tough one to bring up. We figured out that we had both felt expectations from the other for years, and we had "stuffed" them, rather than talk about them, so we both had resentments. We are sorting those out reasonably well.

If I become aware of a resentment now, I begin by asking forgiveness for not bringing up the issue at the time, and then we go about dealing with the feelings. As I have freed myself to deal with resentments, I have also freed myself to feel a broad range of other feelings, including love. It is a joy to be able to unreservedly tell my wife that I know now what love is, and I love her. Better communication about intimate issues, more emotional intimacy and healthier individuals have made for a more satisfying sexual life.

Sharing my fears opened up communication

I grew up in a non-alcoholic home full of trust. I believed people would do what they said when they said it. In this family, however, there was always a concern about making ends meet. This concern was not hidden from me, but I was provided for and given everything I needed. When I entered into a relationship with an alcoholic, who later became my husband, these childhood values continued. I was always baffled when he never had any money to pay for our dates. This should have been a red flag.

After we got married, we had several financial crises because he paid for his booze rather than his bills, but I did not attribute it to alcoholism. As the disease progressed in both my husband and me, our relationship became more like we were roommates, rather than husband and wife. We didn't discuss bills and I began to not buy things for myself so that we would have money to pay the bills. The disease of alcoholism was never discussed.

Eventually I joined Al-Anon. By working with a Sponsor, studying and applying the Steps and Traditions to my life, I realized that I was afraid of financial ruin. Every time my husband drank, I went to the scenario in my mind of being homeless and living on the street.

When I was about seven years into the program, we started asking God into our marriage. We turned our marriage over to God's care. We realized that my husband was probably going to be downsized in his current job, so we started on Plan B. Plan B was to move to another city and start a business from scratch. Oh boy! Did the fear come up in me and give me the feeling of powerlessness. I would now be the sole breadwinner for our family.

Due to the work I had done in Al-Anon, I was able to tell my husband that I had genuine fear about starting this business. The fears were that he would drink again, the business would fail and that we would lose everything. Just saying the fear out loud relieved a lot of it. We decided to pray and include God in the decision. We turned our will and our lives over to a God of our understanding that day. From that moment, my fear was relieved, though it wasn't entirely gone. We made a financial strategy as well as a business strategy to make the move.

This sharing of fear opened up the communication between my husband and myself, and we began to share more personal thoughts with each other. We started showing respect to each other and allowing each other to speak without interruption, which I had learned by studying Concept Five ("The rights of appeal and petition protect minorities and insure that they be heard") and Tradition Two ("For our group purpose there is but one authority—a loving God as He may express Himself in our group conscience. Our leaders are but trusted servants—they do not govern."). Acknowledging my fear to God and another human being (Step Five) gave me freedom and serenity.

Starting a new business was tough and the road was often rocky. Fear came back, but because I could recognize it, I could turn it over and know that God would be with me. Since that night of fear almost 11 years ago, we have moved, run the business, sold it for a profit, stayed sane and had miracles happen that have changed my life.

Honest communication made intimacy possible

My husband and I were married on a day in August 45 years ago. Almost immediately, I felt like something was wrong, but it was another eight years before it had a name: alcoholism. I joined Al-Anon when I was 28. Although he never drank again after joining A.A. a year later, my husband did not stay and participate in meetings, though I stayed in Al-Anon. I felt a lack of intimacy emotionally, spiritually and physically, but I blamed myself: I had married my husband without feeling a physical attraction to him. This was my big secret. I had pretended, but felt more and more guilty that I had misled him. I tried to accommodate him, but sex was at the bottom of my list.

When I learned in Al-Anon that intimacy does not equal sex—that intimacy is sharing who you really are deep inside—it was a revelation to me. So I brought home books with little sharing exercises in them. Many of them were probably excellent for beginning to establish intimacy between two people, but the two people do have to both be willing. My husband was not, and we never got to first base.

I had many more excellent ideas—emphasis on the "I"—none of which worked. We would go to weekend workshops on marriage, but whatever gains we made there were quickly abandoned once we got back home on our own. We saw a minister for counseling, but I don't remember it changing anything. Trying to talk about our relationship was frustrating—it always seemed to end with a lack of understanding between us. We always fell back to talking about our children and their problems. I didn't even share at all about one of the happiest developments in my life—my spiritual awakening in Al-Anon—with my atheistic husband.

It was impossible to build intimacy without honesty. There were other secrets, which by themselves—let alone all of them together!—prevented intimacy: emotional, spiritual, or physical. From time to time we tried spicing up our sex life, but, unsurprisingly, to no lasting effect. My heart really wasn't in it. For many years, I concentrated on raising our three boys.

This is where my story changes. A few years ago, my husband started to regularly attend A.A. meetings. After a particularly awful incident a year ago, I absolutely refused to accept what I felt was unacceptable behavior. It helped me that he had the support of A.A., and I was able to leave him. I will never forget how my Sponsor—it is never too late to get a Sponsor!—welcomed me to her home, moving out of her own bedroom so I could have privacy and my own space. After writing several honest and searching emails to me, my husband asked for a sort of talk therapy with each other, and I agreed to it on a trial basis. I admit I had seen so many false starts in the past, I was convinced this would go nowhere.

But something made a huge difference this time—my husband began by looking me in the eye and saying, "I know you're not physically attracted to me." I can only imagine how much courage it took for him to say that. It took all my courage not to deny it. I looked him back in the eye and told him how dishonest and unfair I felt I had been to him, marrying him under false pretenses. He said, "I always knew. I was afraid if you knew I knew, you would have no reason to stay in the marriage." He was actually convinced it was the end.

Instead, we continued to meet and bring all our feelings about our relationship up slowly, one at a time, over time. It was amazing. Just the agreement to be honest between the two of us, and each week asking, "Do you have anything to talk about?" put new energy into our relationship. We went away from every meeting feeling refreshed, no matter what we brought to it, including feelings like disappointment, resentment and fear. It made a difference that we agreed we needed honesty from each other. We each agreed to act on requests from the other and gave permission to be reminded. We found a neutral place—a hot springs near our house—to go regularly and ask, "Do you have anything to talk about?" We used the rules of conflict resolution. We tried to get our sex life back. That was awkward at times, but at times it was almost playful, and that was new. All of these made the difference.

It has been more than a year now. At one point, we slacked off with our meeting together, only to find that yes, we do need to meet often, probably for the rest of our lives. My Sponsor helped me get over my feelings that there was something wrong with us. She said: "Well, wouldn't it be wonderful if every couple did that? Don't we all need it?"

I feel our relationship finally has the intimacy I always wanted. And the big surprise is, my husband wants it as much as I do. At last, I have no secrets from him, and I feel a new freedom to be myself. I thought I was okay, but now I know I could not grow keeping secrets, and neither could my husband. I feel young again. I like us as a couple. And I find myself with a well of intimate feelings towards others that I never expected. And Al-Anon? It has taken on new life for me. I need it more than ever, and I'm okay with that, too.

We had to argue to be able to grieve

When my father was diagnosed with pancreatic cancer, I came home to take care of my parents. This terrified me. I was scared to watch my father die, but I was also afraid of living with them.

None of us knew how to fight. My father yelled, and my mother and I shut down—until we retaliated, and often tossed the unsuspecting offender out of our lives. Under constant pressure, I feared all of us would be at each other's throats, ruining the months my father had left.

But something had changed: I had worked the Steps. When I moved in with my parents, I wasn't alone. I brought my Step work, my Sponsor, and my group with me. My dad yelled sometimes, and sometimes my mother and I shut down. After he passed, we shut down for months. When she told me she needed me to contribute more, and asked when I was leaving, I shut down with a vengeance, but I knew that solved nothing. Out came my Tenth-Step inventories, the calls to my Tenth-Step partner, and my prayers to my Higher Power, asking for sanity and guidance.

It took three days, but finally I got the go-ahead. I calmed down enough to talk about my grief and what I needed, instead of what she did wrong. It didn't go perfectly—she got defensive at times, as did I—but we needed to argue. We had to work out what had hurt us. Only by talking it out, the way the Steps taught me, could I run toward her, not just run away.

Courteous communication brought us together

As my relationship with my alcoholic husband ran into its eighth year, our intimacy in every area was affected. What surprised me most was that our close sharing started to disappear more than anything else. My focus became only what he was doing rather than sharing loving kindness with him and my daughter. The loss of our sharing was mostly caused by my obsessive behavior with how much he was drinking.

His inappropriate behavior at home and in public was so humiliating, I became fearful of being anywhere with him. At a college football game, he lost his temper with someone and they had a sword fight with umbrellas. I crouched under the seat as much as I could, as did the other spouse. The sword fight lasted for what seemed like ten minutes. When it stopped I could say nothing. I was barely aware that a football game was going on. I did not speak during the four-hour drive home; I pretended to sleep.

I joined Al-Anon shortly after and began my journey back to life. My first attempts at detaching were quiet in sound but loud in the attitude that I was the martyr trying to help our marriage. With help from my Sponsor, I learned to put courtesy back into our family. The smile I used with everyone else, including strangers, I brought back into the house. I gave gratitude to my husband and daughter for everything they were doing in our home.

As I began to change, our family began to change. After a year my husband said, "The Al-Anon way is really helping our family." It was true. Even though he was still drinking, we were working together as a family for the first time in many years. Using the Al-Anon Legacies, we started having family discussions about things we did together. Everyone had input and most of the time we all agreed with our decisions.

We even used inclusion with discipline for our daughter. She was to go to her room and think about what her punishment should be. My husband and I would make a decision on what we felt should happen. At the beginning, our daughter would pick a punishment much more severe than what she had done. Discussing together that the "punishment should fit the crime" gave our daughter a sense of confidence in making behavior choices as well as a strong trust factor that she could share with us and have a trust that we loved her unconditionally, something that neither my husband nor I had felt from our parents.

It took seven more years for my husband to stop drinking and go into treatment, but by then we were already well on our way to developing a family intimacy between the three of us.

Al-Anon is showing me how to listen and share

Intimacy takes careful listening and thoughtful, authentic sharing. I have perhaps learned to do this more in Al-Anon meetings than anywhere else. I love the fact that we don't interrupt each other at my group and that we usually limit our sharing to five minutes each. This helps us to let go of any other thoughts and just listen to each other. We are able to communicate our feelings without blame or shame.

There is a lot of laughter at Al-Anon meetings, especially about the crazy things we have done in reaction to the disease of alcoholism. One Al-Anon member said, "Laughter is the shortest distance between two people." That is so true! In Al-Anon I have learned to laugh at my own mistakes and shortcomings, and this helps me to gradually let them go.

Intimacy involves careful, authentic speaking. It involves staying silent when my thoughts are judgmental and unkind, and waiting until I can speak my truth assertively, but also kindly. It involves reaching out for better connection and cooperation, by expressing my needs respectfully and also listening to the needs of others. I am very grateful that Al-Anon helps me to practice building my intimacy skills.

I learned to accept myself

I felt like the word "different" was stamped on my forehead until I entered the rooms of Al-Anon. When I was 27, I lost my first love, a recovering alcoholic, to AIDS. After he died, I entered into a dark period of my life. I felt so isolated from my immediate family, especially my dad, who disowned me because I am gay.

As countless people have testified, "Al-Anon saved my life." Al-Anon saved my life when my recovery process began as I started to work the Steps with my wonderful Sponsor. With the help of Al-Anon, I am healing in ways I never thought possible.

Today, I prefer appropriate behaviors—hugs, kisses, laughter, crying, sharing and caring—over inappropriate behaviors like yelling insults, hitting and rudeness. God did not place me on Earth to be wounded by others' unhappiness.

Today, I am single. I keep telling myself, "God is still working on that someone special for me." Overall, Al-Anon is healing me in this area of my life. At one meeting, I shared about being the survivor of childhood sexual abuse. After the meeting, several members and friends in Al-Anon showered me with kind words and hugs. I did not feel "different." I felt "special."

Growing up, I learned not to share my most intimate feelings—that men were not supposed to do that. Men were not supposed to be vulnerable. Al-Anon is changing that perception in my life. I am allowed to feel free. I feel safe in Al-Anon and with my Sponsor to share what is in my heart and on my mind. By doing this, I am learning about unconditional love and intimacy. My Al-Anon family accepts me for the person I truly am. My Al-Anon family does for me what my family of origin cannot. It is non-judgmental, loving, kind and caring. I love my Al-Anon family very much.

I had to give what I wanted to get

I notice that when I need a hug or simple affection, I act as if I don't want to be touched or bothered. Interesting, huh?

Then the man that I love started to do this while he was getting sober. I felt as if I should just stay away and give him space. He certainly was putting out energy of "don't touch me." But my Higher Power gave me this question: "What do I need when I am pushing people away?" The answer came: connection, love and kindness. So I started to ask for a hug.

In this way, he could say no and I wouldn't take it personally. I know what it is like to have someone put their affection on me when I don't want it. It feels overwhelming to me, impersonal, and like a big intrusion. So, asking if I can have a hug and letting go of the outcome worked. If he said yes to a hug and was sitting down I started to sit on him and give him a big bear hug. At first I felt uncomfortable doing this and I saw that he did too. We had so many arguments, disagreements, disconnection with each other throughout our relationship that being affectionate with each other in this effortless way almost felt wrong. It was certainly uncomfortable, but I had to trust my Higher Power and the message.

Over the years we have found our simple ways to connect. We like to hold hands. Neither of us knew this until one of us (not sure which one of us) asked to hold hands as we walked down the street. Soon this became our practice, to ask the other and now we always say yes and tend to hold hands a lot more than we did. I also feel this is a good example to our daughter.

Asking for what we need and showing simple affection for each other daily is a great reminder to us that we have love for each other. I now enjoy when we disagree on a subject, because at some point, even though we have not come to a solution, one of us will ask for a hug. This always warms my heart and puts me in a space of realizing it isn't the outcome that is important, it is the journey and whether I am showing up in connection, love and kindness.

Questions for Reflection

1. In what ways am I in touch with my thoughts and feelings? In which situations do I have more difficulty determining what I think or feel?

2. When do I feel comfortable expressing my thoughts and feelings? In what situations is this more difficult for me? What makes it easier?

3. When I share my thoughts and feelings with others, what kind of response would I most like to get? What happens when I get a response I don't want?

4. With which people in my life am I most comfortable sharing? With whom do I find it the most difficult to communicate?

5. How do I communicate how I feel to those I love? How does this compare to how I express myself at meetings?

6. When others are sharing at meetings, what am I usually doing? How does this compare to my behavior when others in my life are talking to me?

7. What are some ways I can "keep my side of the street clean" when it comes to my relationships?

8. What happens when I disagree with someone I care about? How does this affect the way I communicate?

9. Which Al-Anon tools can I use to negotiate a disagreement with someone else? How can I show kindness and compassion to others, even when we disagree?

Intimacy in Alcoholic Relationships

Chapter Four
Negotiating Boundaries

Setting boundaries is the foundation for having a healthy relationship with anyone: family members, friends, intimate partners, even ourselves. And yet, before we came to Al-Anon, many of us had no idea what healthy boundaries looked like. The disease of alcoholism gave us warped senses of what was acceptable behavior, as these Al-Anon members share:

- "To him, regular 'vanilla' sex was boring. He wanted sex encumbered with costumes, games and elaborate sex toys; membership in clubs where polyamory was the norm. I went along with it all to please him. I never asked myself if this lifestyle was right for me."

- "Both my parents were embarrassed by any affection openly shown—whether it was a hug, a kiss or even a compliment."

- "When he was drunk, my father would cross boundaries of sexual intimacy that he wouldn't cross sober. This included sexual molestation. When I became old enough to tell him to stop, he stopped all displays of affection. This led to my feeling that in order to get affection I had to give all or get nothing."

- "I thought my husband's love and attention defined my self-worth."

- "Eventually, sexual relations became very much like social situations had become: unpredictable, dangerous, something to be avoided. I dreaded the moment when my wife would come home from the bar, never knowing if she would be angry, abusive, sexually aggressive or all three."

- "I was taught to share a public persona that did not reveal our family's secrets—good, bad or indifferent. Within our home, we learned not to divulge certain feelings or opinions with one another. I never discussed the anger I felt towards family members or the fear and shame that overwhelmed me."

- "If we did hold each other at all, it always led to sex."

- "In my home of origin, intimacy was always forced and almost always unwanted. It was treated like a God-given right by the alcoholic. Neither we children nor my mother seemed to want to be close to him, yet the message was clear that we needed him for survival. We were financially dependent on someone I did not trust."

In our efforts to find love and acceptance, we often looked to others in order to determine how we should think, feel and behave. As one member shares, "I lived my life like a chameleon, changing my personality to suit the group of people around me." Unfortunately, this behavior produced exactly the opposite of what we had hoped to achieve: Instead of feeling loved and accepted, we felt a keen disconnect between who we really were and how we had presented ourselves to others. When taken to its extreme, looking to others for our peace of mind led some of us to lose ourselves entirely in the relationship. By constantly focusing on others' preferences, we forgot our own likes and dislikes. We took on responsibilities that did not belong to us, and neglected our own. We could no longer tell where we ended and others began.

Others of us, however, took the opposite road, choosing instead to cut ourselves off from people as much as possible to avoid being hurt. One Al-Anon member shares how this reaction backfired:

"Living with the insanity of alcoholism, I redoubled my protections, building impenetrable castle walls for self-preservation. Unfortunately, this prohibited me from experiencing intimacy in any way—including from my Higher Power. Love no longer flowed in or out: it stagnated and festered, and I blamed the alcoholics. My attitudes and beliefs kept me protected and separated from humanity. I was alone, starving for affection, connection, attention and real intimacy—that is, love."

When we come to Al-Anon, we encounter a healthy boundary, perhaps for the first time in our lives, in the Suggested Al-Anon Welcome: That "it is possible for us to find contentment, and even happiness, whether the alcoholic is still drinking or not." Practicing detachment with love is a key component to learning how to live life on our own terms. For some of us, the detachment was the difficult part, and for others, it was "with love." Whether we were too involved or uninvolved, use of the slogans, the Twelve Steps and Twelve Traditions can help us determine for ourselves what is and is not acceptable behavior, from ourselves as well as from other people in our lives.

The Fourth and Fifth Steps, in particular, can help us sort out our boundaries. Taking a searching and fearless moral inventory of ourselves (Step Four) and then sharing the results with a Higher Power and a Sponsor or other trusted person (Step Five) allows us to see which behaviors and attitudes helped us, and which harmed us. Knowing what is good for us and what is not is the first step in establishing healthy limits for ourselves, inside and outside of relationships.

Once we know what our boundaries are, there still remains the problem of setting and keeping them. After years of trying to please others, we may find it awkward to speak up for our own needs and desires. In the context of sexual relationships, many of us felt that acceding to sex was our duty, whether we wanted to or not.

That is not to say that we have the right to regulate other people's behavior. Boundaries are for our own safety and protection, and are our responsibility. Expecting our wants and needs to override anyone else's is not setting boundaries, but an effort to control or manipulate others. Just as we cannot make someone be honest with us, we cannot force another person to accommodate our needs at the expense of their own. If someone in our lives is incapable of being emotionally supportive of us, for instance, then demanding emotional support from them is a futile effort. In Al-Anon, we learn to take responsibility for making sure our own needs are met.

Having an intimate relationship, however, requires that everyone in the relationship benefit from it. This is where negotiating boundaries comes in. If we have built trust and can communicate clearly and freely within the relationship, then we have the tools necessary to determine together what is most comfortable, supportive and desirable for each person involved. This applies to any kind of relationship: romantic partners, parents and children, siblings, friends or even ourselves.

Luckily, in Al-Anon we learn that we have choices. If others overstep our boundaries, whether or not we have stated them out loud, we can choose to remove ourselves from the situation. As we learn to recognize unsafe situations, we may find that we develop strategies for not getting into them in the first place. If we do find ourselves in dire straits despite our best efforts, we have the tools of the Al-Anon program to help us out again.

Members Share Experience, Strength and Hope

I can set limits that are comfortable for me

I knew I had problems with intimacy even before I came to Al-Anon eight years ago. When trying to make friends, I used to stay and stay and stay, trying to force it and fake it. I felt depleted for weeks afterwards and vowed never to go back.

Immersing myself in the Al-Anon program, I worked the Steps actively with a Sponsor and attended lots of meetings. This gave me room and time to slowly understand how to be me. I began to practice being my own friend and chief nurturer. I gradually began to not be so anxious to make instant friends, or have to be seen with others to feel safe, like I had friends.

I think it is no coincidence that a few months after completing Step Twelve I had an intense desire to begin working the Traditions—and what are the Traditions for, but working with each other? I began to realize I had no idea of the basic concepts of friendship. My Sponsor encouraged me to use Al-Anon literature, which evolved into looking up "relationship" in the index of the book *How Al-Anon Works for Families & Friends of Alcoholics* (B-32). I began reading the stories in the second half of the book. I had purchased the book when I first came to Al-Anon, but reading the stories now with a history of recovery made them so real and precious to me.

Reading all these stories helped me see why I preferred isolation to the messiness of having no boundaries or ground rules for relationships. I discovered that I don't have to decide to help others impulsively. I can take my time to figure out—with my Higher Power's help—how I'm going to respond. Now I can give an hour or two of my time "for fun and for free" to friends and other acquaintances, and when my little clock says the hour is up, tell them goodbye and wish them a great day.

I can choose not to be intimate if I don't feel safe

I find now, or rather I notice now, that my ability or willingness to be intimate depends on my feeling safe with the other person. In the past, before Al-Anon, I unconsciously believed I had a duty to be sexual with my partner—that being in a relationship meant I should be willing whenever the other person wanted to be sexually intimate (unless I was really ill). The result was that I had sex when I did not want to, when I needed to rest, when I didn't feel safe, when I did not feel kindly toward my partner, even when it physically hurt.

Now, in recovery, I don't "have to." This is so amazing—it means I don't traumatize myself by being intimate when I am not ready to do so. If my husband and I have argued, I may say, "I am still in the argument, I don't feel safe right now," and opt not to be intimate. I also talk with my Sponsor about these matters—we have talked about my past trauma and about having "safe sex," meaning spiritually, emotionally safe in addition to physically safe.

I had to set boundaries to show love and respect

Growing up with an alcoholic father, I had often felt alone, unsafe and unsure of his love. Sometimes he was barely present when I needed his attention. Sometimes he demanded my attention when he was needy. It was all very confusing. I remember making the commitment that I would never allow my own children to ever be in doubt about my love for them. I would make sure that they received in abundance what I had lacked during my own childhood.

How did that work for me? Not very well. My oldest daughter quickly learned that Daddy had a hard time saying "no." When she asked for an ice cream cone, I was glad to say "yes." Then she would ask if it could be a sugar cone. Two scoops? Then could she have it chocolate dipped? Then she wanted sprinkles on top. Wherever I would finally draw a limit, whether at the beginning or after several additional requests, she pouted in her disappointment. She acted as though I was not being generous. She looked unloved.

It took several years of working the Al-Anon program before I was able to see that I was giving my daughter the power to decide whether I was being a loving parent. I had abandoned all measures within myself regarding whether I was loving her. Nothing I did was good enough unless she "felt loved." I was giving her what I had wanted, and she was using it to lead me around like a bull with a ring through my nose.

The truth was that I did know somewhere inside that I loved her, but I was ignoring what I knew. As a result, I resented my daughter's constant requests to show her my love. I was putting her into a difficult bind—showering her with endless acts of "love" from a place of resentment. No wonder she was confused about me.

Al-Anon helped me begin paying more attention to my own internal standards. In discussions with other trusted members and increasing contact with my Higher Power, I began to develop confidence in my own feelings. I began to trust that my daughter would be able to see my love and devotion to her even when I set boundaries that disappointed her.

The first test of our relationship came when my wife and I put our daughter into treatment for her use of alcohol and other drugs. She did not like that at the time, but thanks us today. We all soon learned that recovery involves more than merely abstaining from alcohol. And recovery for those who love an alcoholic involves more than no longer enabling their drinking. I still had to learn how to abstain from letting my daughter be the judge of how much I loved her.

I stopped paying many of her bills and told her that she had become a clever young woman, able to figure out how to earn the money she needed to take care of her own needs. I was no longer taking over her responsibilities in her own life, and over time she began to understand that this did not mean that I loved her less. It meant that I respected her more.

Today we both feel more secure in our love for each other than any time in the past. I no longer let her determine whether I love her. I know I do, and I trust that this comes through in the respect I show for her freedom to follow her own path. We were able to deepen our intimacy only when I stopped trying to buy her love and approval—when I was able to be content with taking care of my own business and allowing my daughter to make decisions for herself.

I established a boundary—and kept it

Intimacy has sometimes been a struggle for me because I suffered sexual and physical abuse as a child at the hands of my alcoholic father. I married a man in recovery in the hopes that sobriety would be the foundation of our marriage, but my husband relapsed a few months into the relationship, right after I discovered I was pregnant.

I made an internal vow, that no matter how much I desired physical intimacy, I would not make love to my husband if he'd been drinking. This decision led to arguments, some of them volatile, with pushing and swearing on his part, but I never yielded. This boundary was too important to me.

Although sex was rare—perhaps once a month, instead of frequently, which I would have preferred—it was a treasured experience. These little breaks of sweetness and tenderness were islands on a sea of uncertainty.

My now ex-husband and I co-parent two teenagers, and he has been sober for several years after serving time in jail for multiple DUIs. I am not only grateful for his sobriety, and my Al-Anon program, but for the memories I cherish, of love shown and received during difficult days. I would never judge another's choice—to abstain from sex entirely, or to accept intimacy with a drinking partner—but the choice I made was right for me.

The solution to my struggle was a familiar one

One of the most important intimate relationships in my life is with my brother. We are close in age, only 18 months apart. We shared, and still share, many of the same interests. As children in an alcoholic home, we often shared a bed to cope with our nighttime fears.

It took me a long time in Al-Anon to acknowledge the importance of this relationship, and how it was damaged through a shared alcoholic upbringing. To this day, we have trouble showing affection. A recent postcard from my brother expressed his love for me. He later admitted he was drunk when he sent it.

For all the years I struggled with this relationship, it turned out the solution was the same for us brothers as it was for all my family relationships: I shared at a meeting about my struggles with my brother, my fear that he is an alcoholic, and my frustration that I couldn't cure him. Some members hugged me, others thanked me for my very deep sharing, while others suggested I could pray for him. I cried, then prayed for him.

God has since sent me a renewed relationship with my brother. He is more open with me, and I am learning to accept him for who he is. I had been angry that God and Al-Anon could solve a problem I could not. Sharing at meetings has helped me resolve that anger, too. Now I am free to love my brother, admit how close we are, and how important he is to me. We remain intimate, even if we never choose to discuss our upbringing. I love him for who he is, thanks to this loving fellowship and my Al-Anon family.

My relationships are my responsibility

When I came to Al-Anon I truly struggled with dating and long-term relationships. My relationships were short-lived, and I often felt hurt and wounded by these experiences. I was quick to blame others for my struggles in this area. I believed my parents hadn't taught me how to relate to others and, as a result, the men I dated treated me poorly.

In Al-Anon I found wise members and helpful literature which advised me to keep the focus on myself and examine my own behavior. Very, very slowly, over much time I was able to gather healthier tools for communication, as well as get in touch with my feelings, set boundaries and develop greater self-respect. I began to let go of blame and practice "Live and Let Live."

I came to realize that, as a grown man, my behavior and all my relationships were totally my responsibility and that change was possible. I have since experienced wonderful changes in all my relationships, including family, friends, colleagues and a life-partner.

We took a slow and careful approach to our relationship

My story of "intimacy in the alcoholic relationship" is a bit different than most, since I met my partner after she had a few years of A.A. recovery and shortly after she came out as lesbian. We both had a series of previous failed relationships that were short and abusive, lacking both trust and intimacy. Thus, we approached our relationship slowly and carefully.

Due to lack of trust on both our parts from these past relationships, I was willing to listen to one of her A.A. friends, who suggested we write a "what we want out of our relationship" contract. Since change is part of everyone's cycle of life, we have updated this contract time and again. However, a few items have remained at the top of the list. For example, we agreed to take care of our own recovery programs; we are committed to a monogamous relationship and we work diligently to keep the lines of communication open—specifically in the areas of intimacy and sexual creativity, finances and overall work/life balance.

Working with Alateens gave me an unexpected gift

I got married in my 40s to a man with six children ranging in age from eight to 22. When we took in several of them for a period of time, I was faced with the challenge of developing relationships with teenagers and young adults.

A few years before this, in a move I now see as guided by my Higher Power, I had been invited into Alateen service when I never thought I would choose to work with teenagers. I was terrified of them! I had not had an easy adolescence and in some ways had been stuck in the negative feelings and poor self-image I developed in my own teen years. Becoming an Alateen Sponsor, and later serving on the committee in my Area that developed Alateen requirements, was a journey of healing. I learned to love my own inner teenager, and freed myself to love Alateens and teenagers in general.

Now I had the opportunity to apply my recovery to intimate personal relationships with my stepchildren. As a new stepmother, I wanted to get to know them and have healthy interactions, but the inner guidance I received was to let the relationships unfold naturally without "forcing solutions." I made myself available and let them lead the way. I kept practicing my program so that I continued to grow and evolve, and I put principles into action when given the chance to have conversations on intimate topics, such as life goals and plans, emotional upsets and dilemmas, and dealing with difficult relationships and interactions. Slowly my stepchildren grew to trust me.

It wasn't all smooth sailing, for sure; we had our share of conflict, and sometimes that created conflict between my partner and me. But because of my commitment to practicing Al-Anon principles, I was able to weather the storms, keep my sanity and hold a steady course with my stepchildren, staying open, honest and willing to listen, share and be there for them.

With my middle stepdaughter, we started out talking about her interests—video games, TV, people and relationships—and slowly eased into more emotional depths. The true test of intimacy with her came a few years later, when she ran into some deep despair and self-hatred, to the point of becoming suicidal. There were several incidents of crucial decisions for her, when I was able to intercept her before she harmed herself, and she allowed me to help her process through and release the urge to act on her thoughts. It took patience, and all the Al-Anon tools at my disposal. I was able to stay calm, detach with love and not force solutions. Instead, I simply listened and offered love and help as she made her way out of the darkness. I am grateful that today she is happy and healthy, and I am honored she let me help her in the dark times.

Today, with all my stepchildren, I do my best to live by spiritual principles, to stay away from trying to control, and to offer suggestions only if asked. It is a joy to have close relationships with several of my stepchildren, especially those who want to share feelings, process life events, and ask for support and guidance.

I made a list of qualities I was looking for in a partner

When I was ready to begin dating, I had a lot of fear. I read in *Courage to Change* (B-16) about making three amends lists—

one for people to whom I will definitely make amends, one for those I might make amends to, and one for people to whom I will not be making amends.

I used that suggestion and made three lists of characteristics for a person I would want a relationship with. The first list was of qualities that were mandatory in a relationship. This list included: having a spiritual program of some kind, giving back to society monetarily or through time and being financially responsible. The second list included qualities that were deal-breakers: I didn't want to be with someone who smoked, took drugs or drank alcoholically. The third list had conditional items. If the person were an alcoholic, she would need to have a minimum of five years of sobriety, have a Sponsor and have worked through Step Five. If there was anything on the deal-breaker list, the relationship would be over. No exceptions.

I wrote the list down, so there would be no cheating on my part. I really didn't think anyone would qualify! Then I met the woman who has now been my partner for ten years. She met every quality on the must-have list. She had none of the qualities on the deal-breaker list or on the conditional list.

I am with someone who shares a similar spiritual path. We both believe in giving to others—I through Al-Anon, she through organizations that are important to her. We each want the other to be the best woman she can be. Because our relationship has a spiritual foundation, we share a level of intimacy that I have not experienced in previous relationships.

Keeping my side of the street clean

Being married to an alcoholic can feel incredibly one-sided. When I rely on my husband for emotional support or to fulfill my intimate needs, I often am left rejected and empty. If I let these feelings continue without awareness, my resentments grow. My Al-Anon family and Higher Power have taken on the role of fulfilling my emotional support. They have provided a nurturing, non-judgmental and loving place for me whenever I need something or someone to lean on.

The intimate needs are the one piece that cannot be met by anyone other than my husband. I wish that I felt desired—that he would want to pounce and make love to me, but he doesn't. If he were sick in bed with the flu, I wouldn't expect him to be intimate with me. I need to keep this perspective of his disease controlling our intimate life rather than his lack of desire for me and our relationship.

I also know that I need to keep my side of the street clean. I have decided to continue the commitment I made at our wedding and do not want to resort to infidelity to fulfill those needs. I realize now that his lack of affection is not about me at all, just like his anger and blame have nothing to do with me. I have to turn over my relationship to my Higher Power. The only thing that I have control over is my attitude and personal wellness. By practicing the program, I have the strength to believe that I am still desirable and lovable—with or without my significant other.

In spite of my fear, I started asking for change

Needing another person to feel okay killed intimacy for me. This was my legacy from growing up in an alcoholic home. Mine wasn't an addiction to just one person: I found both a father figure in my boss at work, and a mother figure in my wife at home. I allowed both of them to control me, and systematically denied myself.

I was highly skilled at my work but could never advance because I could not pursue my own interests; I couldn't even insist on getting paid regularly. I could have been a good husband, too: For example, I had a weekly consultation with my wife (no kids, no time limit, no imposed agenda), but both at home and work I lacked the wisdom—and gumption—to know I had to be personally present as well. Instead, in both places, I simply agreed to everything that my wife and my boss asked for, wanted or demanded.

They wanted more and more. As their demands expanded, they came into conflict with each other. They became rivals. Each wanted my complete self-sacrifice on his or her sole behalf. Trying to please not one but two insatiable masters put an extreme stress on me. Living within that tension suffocated me, wearing me to a thread.

I didn't completely lose my moral compass, but I sure perverted it. I thought I was doing the right thing. I convinced myself that it was both spiritual and honorable to say to them, over and over, "Yes, sure, I'll get that done" or "Yes, I'll do my best to do that." I didn't consider myself a coward; I thought it took a lot of spiritual strength to keep trying harder to do the "right thing" when, over and over, it didn't work. In retrospect, I see I was spending all my energy trying to change the things I couldn't, and saving none for taking responsibility for myself. I had "Let Go and Let God" all mixed up!

As my sickness progressed over decades, the only thing I was looking to for strength was how I thought these two people perceived me. "I" had completely disappeared; I had no friends, hobbies or interests. I took no vacations. As an independent person, I was not only absent from these foundational relationships but also from my own perception of myself. My unhappiness increased, and I became suicidal. Finally, I reached the breaking point. In visualizing my death, I felt I had already died, and imagined having a very uncomfortable conversation with God about rejecting His gift of life.

Avoiding that conversation with God would require me to try something new. After six months in Al-Anon, I found the wisdom to start asking for change, both at home and at work. I was terrified. The first time I sent my boss an email saying I would not be around so much anger (a polite way of saying emotional abuse), I felt all color and life drain out of my mental picture of life. In that instant, in my mind's eye, the whole world became a post-nuclear-war wasteland with a dry wind blowing the dust.

It took me longer to initiate boundaries at home, but I did. And after about two years of working my program in Al-Anon, I left both home and work within three months of each other. I was homeless, jobless and moneyless, with no religious community (they had both dominated me there, too). I had begun the great journey of trying to get my own needs met. I was finally taking responsibility for myself. It was not pretty; it was, in fact, messy. There wasn't much to "me," but what there was, was finally real.

I learned that I didn't really need the approval of either boss or wife, father or mother. I learned that what I really did need was the approval of my Higher Power—which had been there all along! All I had to do was ask. Now I have the potential for intimacy. I have something—some "me"—to offer. I do not act helpless as a means of winning approval. I am learning to tell the truth about how I feel. I can name many of the things that bother me. I can tell you what I want. I have intimate relationships in which we can share anything—I think that's what you call friendships! I like myself for the first time in my life. Foregoing the need for approval of any fixed person or people has freed me to be myself, which has ironically resulted in more approval from many more people.

Even more important to me is my growth in intimacy with my Higher Power. I tell the truth to God, too, and listen to His will much better than I did before. Of course, I am still inclined to find somebody to put on a pedestal and define myself by his or her approval. But I am increasingly protected both by a sense of revulsion when I behave that way, and by the kind of people I now seek out as friends. They don't like that behavior either. They'll often tell me even before I see myself doing it. That's part of intimacy, too.

I look at every incident in which I try to make someone else responsible for me as a chance to exercise Al-Anon principles. If I keep going to the meetings and working my program, I cannot help getting into better shape. For I have seen the unconditional love of God shining through the faces of my friends, and sometimes, now, even through my own face in the mirror. I would not trade this growth for anything in the world.

I made a decision based solely on taking care of myself

I have chronic hepatitis C. I promised myself that I would request any partner I became intimate with to get tested for all sexually transmitted diseases, as I would myself. This would be our commitment to our relationship and give us a foundation from which to begin our sexual intimacy. I practiced this diligently until I met my alcoholic partner. Delusional thinking allowed me to begin a sexual relationship without him getting tested. My good sense to protect my health disappeared with his insistent charm of "knowing" he was "healthy and clean." I was deeply active in my own disease, but at least I insisted that we used condoms. I was trying to protect myself from any sexually transmitted infection I could still contract.

Next, I asked him to get tested out of my concern for *his* health. He came up with all possible excuses why he couldn't—fear of needles, cost and so on. I researched solutions for him that would allow him to get tested anonymously and even for free.

With genuine concern and love for him, and guilt that I may be contributing to his early death, I was still trying to control our relationship and him. My self-respect eroded over time.

We broke up and got back together several times in the next two years, but nine months of attending Al-Anon and working the Steps helped me grow stronger. I lived with peace and serenity more often than not, and learned to value myself and my health. I slowly relearned to be responsible to and for myself.

As our relationship progressed, we both wanted to stop using condoms. Six months ago, at our most recent reconciliation, I set a boundary—no intercourse unless he got tested. This time I based my decision solely on taking care of myself. I reminded myself that my immune system is compromised, and though overall healthy, I must protect my health. I knew that the responsibility of making informed decisions rested with me.

He continues to try to wear down my boundary, but respects my decision when I say "no" or "get tested." When I indicate he is crossing the line, he now responds, "Yes, I know I need to get tested." I am able to smile and teasingly say, "You're right." Our bedroom intimacy has progressed downward from enjoyable intercourse to quick lip pecks and infrequent cuddling.

He has yet to get tested. I miss our sexual intimacy. These may all be indicators that our relationship is slowly coming to an end...or not. I don't know. I do know we are both making conscious decisions. I also know that in my Al-Anon journey I am saner than before. I am happier now that I am re-establishing my self-determination. I am regaining my self-respect and integrity.

I learned I didn't have to participate

Before I joined Al-Anon, I was confronted with inappropriate sexual behavior and I didn't know how to deal with it. My husband subscribed to a TV porn channel. He said, "It's something for both of us to enjoy." I told him, "I'm not into it." He ignored my remark. As we sat in front of the TV one evening, he put the porn channel on and proceeded to watch. I hated it. It made me sick to watch it. My husband would look over and say, "I know you are enjoying this." I responded, "No, I am not!" but I didn't take any further action. I just sat there.

Then after years of putting up with my husband's heavy drinking and hard partying, I finally came to Al-Anon in despair, anger and resentment. There I learned I have choices. An Al-Anon member told me, "If you are in an environment that is making you feel unhappy and unsafe, then leave and go to a place where you feel safe." This was truly a revolutionary idea. Such a simple solution as this never occurred to me.

The next time my husband put the porn channel on, I got up from the couch and went to our bedroom and read a book. He came into the room and asked me why I wasn't out there with him. I told him, "I am not interested in watching this channel. I don't like it. But feel free to watch it without me." Shortly after, when he realized that he couldn't get me to watch it with him, my husband unsubscribed from the channel.

This happened two months after I joined Al-Anon. It was my very first miracle and my first step in setting a boundary and taking care of myself. I am very grateful to Al-Anon and for all the tools it has given me: The Serenity Prayer, the Twelve Steps and Traditions, the slogans and members' experience, strength and hope. All of these tools have given me the courage to change.

Doing a Fifth Step helped me set boundaries for myself

Sitting in Al-Anon meetings, hearing people share their feelings, experiences and situations touched a place in me. I was not familiar with that touch, and yet it helped. I left feeling better. Over time I was able to get the courage to ask for a Sponsor and do the Steps. When we did the Fifth Step ("Admitted to God, to ourselves, and to another human being the exact nature of our wrongs") and she could relate to my sexual transgressions, I felt an acceptance that freed me from my old ideas of what a person should be. Instead, I started to look at the person I was, and to begin to think about the person I wanted to be.

This focus led me to acknowledge a feeling I had for a married woman. I felt I had run into a dilemma. I talked with a wise friend of mine, and she said, "You can acknowledge the feeling and not act upon it." Learning this helped to start building friendships in Al-Anon, and to not worry if I liked the person too much. This opened my heart tremendously, and the walls I had been hiding behind began to come down. More love flowed into my life, and I was willing to love back.

I finally realized I could only control myself

We were a perfect couple and I was head over heels in love at 16. We were married shortly after I graduated high school. I thought my marriage was great. He drank a little sometimes and we had a few disagreements here and there, but what marriage doesn't have a few rough spots?

I believed I should be submissive to my husband on the issue of sexual intimacy. No one forced it on me initially. Whatever he wanted, whenever he wanted it, I fulfilled it. I maintained this attitude and response for nearly 40 years, but over the years my anger and resentment grew. I didn't know why, but it was there, it was building, and it was getting explosive.

Although sex could be great for both of us, his idea of a good sex life was being intimate eight to ten times a week. The sheer frequency was strangling me. Even if I desperately needed sleep, I learned early on that I would get more sleep if I caved in at two or three in the morning and let him have his way. If I didn't, he would pester me all night. If I tried to avoid him, I would be punished. The more I gave, the more he felt entitled to receive.

I not only didn't know how to set healthy boundaries, I didn't know what healthy boundaries were. I needed space in our intimate relationships and didn't know that I was worthy of choices. Al-Anon helped me see that I do have choices and understand healthy boundaries. I learned that "no" is an acceptable answer and also a complete sentence. Even though I began to understand these principles, it was a long time before I felt worthy of choices—and a much longer time before I had the courage to apply those principles.

My denial was deep—denial of the alcoholism (*Everyone likes to have a bit of fun*), domestic violence (*I made him angry and caused the problem*) and sexual intimacy (*Every man expects— and demands—sex eight to ten times per week*). It took a long time before I began to see that there wasn't a healthy balance in our relationship in any of those areas. As the problem of alcoholism increased over the years, so did the domestic violence and frequency of sexual intimacy.

Our relationship was spinning out of control and I finally realized I could only control myself. Our marriage became explosive when I began to take care of myself. I knew I had to get out for my own sanity and safety. The loss of my marriage, however, was devastating; he was my life, my love, my dreams. My grief was immense. I found tremendous help in the book *Opening Our Hearts, Transforming Our Losses* (B-29) and also from the compassion and fellowship of my Al-Anon friends. Although I had to go through tremendous pain to get to a place of healing, today I am a healthy and happy person because I no longer live in fear and anger from the stress issues in my life that I couldn't control.

Questions for Reflection

1. How do I determine what is right for me?

2. How flexible are my boundaries?

3. When I have difficulty determining my boundaries, what tools can I use to help me decide?

4. How do I express my boundaries to those around me?

5. What do I do when my boundaries conflict with what others in my life want?

6. Which Al-Anon tools help me the most when I'm dealing with other people? With myself?

7. In what areas of my life do I have the most difficulty setting my boundaries?

8. In what circumstances am I most likely to change a decision, if pressured?

9. How do I show respect for others' boundaries?

10. In what situations do I have difficulty respecting others' boundaries?

Chapter Five
Spiritual Solutions

In a program that has no "do's" or "musts," spiritual solutions can be hard to define. We are perhaps far more used to thinking of practical solutions to our problems, such as asking for help or saying "no" when we mean "no." Even making use of the Steps, slogans and other Al-Anon tools can seem more straightforward than spiritual.

Al-Anon is, however, a spiritual program. All the actions we take—reading literature, attending meetings, working with a Sponsor, giving service to the group—are contributing to our recovery and nurturing our spiritual well-being. As we learn, we begin to change. Those of us who were fearful of change come to accept and perhaps even welcome it as a sign of our continuing recovery. Where we felt lonely and isolated, we come to feel less alone and more connected to those around us.

Eventually, that feeling of interconnectedness with others in our lives may develop into feelings of spiritual intimacy, of feeling safe to share who we are with others, and being able to accept them for who they are as well. This is the possibility described in the Suggested Al-Anon Closing, that "though you may not like all of us, you'll love us in a very special way—the same way we already love you." As we practice and learn to trust this spiritual intimacy—with ourselves, our Higher Power and with other human beings—we gain confidence in our ability to let others know the real "us" without losing ourselves to the relationship. The more we practice the principles of the Al-Anon program, the deeper our understanding of ourselves grows, and the more spiritual we become.

Here are a few members' experiences with spiritual growth and intimacy:

- "I have never been a joiner, never part of a group, but I could no longer carry this burden by myself. In Al-Anon I see and hear hope, and I feel a spiritual presence that I have been looking for."

- "Over time, I became more and more open to my Higher Power's desire for my full participation in my own body, life and feelings."

- "Now I am alone, but I am not lonely. During this journey, I found my greatest relationship with God."

- "Today I think of my relationship as a triangle: God is at the top, and my partner and I are the sides of the triangle."

- "Intimacy means that I am learning to 'dig deep' into my being, sharing honestly from that place and then being as compassionate with myself as God is with me."

- "Do I want to look deep inside myself and see who I am? Do I want to share my deep thoughts with my adult children? When I answer truthfully, I discover a lot of fear."

- "When I put my recovery at the top, I can then open myself up to my lovers. By keeping the focus on my spirituality, I create space for the various tools of the program that enable me to engage in deeper and truer relationships."

- "Today, in addition to my daily practice of prayer and meditation, I go on extended retreat times with my Higher Power for two to three days about every six weeks, to deepen my conscious contact with Her."

- "God kept giving me platonic relationships until I was mature enough and healed enough for sex, too."

- "I'm at the beginning of this journey, but because of the Step work I have done with my Sponsor, I am no longer trying to blame the other party or escape into a fantasy land."

- "When I am intimate with my Higher Power, I change, and all my relationships change."

- "Al-Anon has taught me to have a relationship with God—and myself—until I become healthy enough to attract a healthier partner in my life."

- "When I came to my Fourth Step it became clear how I had misused my God-given gift of physical intimacy to satisfy my own self-centered fear that I just wasn't enough. It was then that I started praying to God to help me shape a new sexual ideal."

- "A total surrender to God's will for me in all my relationships is an intimate choice I make today. This decision enhances my self-esteem, feelings of trust, love and a joyous willingness to become involved with the process of living."

- "I have had a Higher Power, Sponsors, the Steps, Traditions—a path to direct me into closer fellowship with friends. I have a communion with them that I feel my Higher Power has with me."

- "I have begun writing a letter to my Higher Power daily, and then answering my letter as I feel my Higher Power would respond. It is amazing to me when I read back what I have written on both sides, that when my Higher Power is writing to me, it is slower, more loving and I get a lot of confidence in myself from reading it."

- "Because of Al-Anon and A.A., my husband and I have started saying our nightly prayers together. I found it to be scary and very uncomfortable at first—it is even more intimate than intercourse. It is bringing us even closer and closer to our Higher Power."

Many of us come into Al-Anon with either a warped view of ourselves, or no sense of self at all. As one member tells it, "The most confronting thing that my Higher Power has revealed to me is that I have not loved or known myself." Many program tools, especially making a fearless and searching moral inventory of ourselves (Step Four) and sharing the exact nature of our wrongs with a Sponsor or other trusted person (Step Five) can help us to see ourselves as we are, and to accept ourselves, perhaps for the first time in our lives. When we can truly accept ourselves in all our imperfections, we will be able to share ourselves with others. Loving ourselves allows us to treat other people in a loving and compassionate way—and, in turn, receive love, compassion and understanding.

Getting to know a person takes time, including when that person is ourselves. Paying attention to our needs and feelings is an important part of that process. Doing something every day to take care of our physical well-being—getting enough rest, exercising, even getting a haircut or a manicure—can help us build trust with ourselves.

Building a relationship with a Higher Power can bring its own challenges. Feelings of low self-worth can make it difficult to accept the concept of a Higher Power, if we feel we don't deserve such attention or care. It is often the loving acceptance and fellowship with other members of Al-Anon that provides us with the first taste of what a relationship with a Power greater than ourselves can feel like.

Steps One, Two and Three help us build a spiritual foundation. Step One ("We admitted we were powerless over alcohol—that our lives had become unmanageable") encourages us to accept that by ourselves we were not able to cope with our problems. Steps Two ("Came to believe that a Power greater than ourselves could restore us to sanity") and Three ("Made a decision to turn our will and our lives over to the care of God *as we understood Him*") help us develop a concept of a Higher Power upon whom we may rely. It is this foundation that gives us the ability to find spiritual solutions to our difficulties in intimate relationships. Once we let go of trying to make our relationships be what we think we want or need, we can allow them to grow and develop under a Higher Power's care.

Following the guidance of a Higher Power can help ease our way through relationships as they begin, change and end. No matter what our concept of a Higher Power may be, letting go of the outcomes in our relationships can release us from feelings of responsibility from everything except our part. The more we take care of ourselves and focus on our own recovery, the more able we are to fully participate in all of our relationships. The more we know and love ourselves, the greater our ability to give love—and receive it. We become more free to be ourselves in every situation, including sexual relationships. As one member shares, "The more spiritual I become, the more I want to have an intimate sexual relationship."

The thought of admitting a Higher Power into our intimate sexual relations may not seem to make sense at first. Many of us came into Al-Anon with the idea that the spiritual and the physical were two separate things. Feelings of guilt and shame about our bodies and around the idea of sex itself might cause us to shy away from the notion of letting a Higher Power into our sexual relationships. For others, such a concept simply sounds absurd.

In practicing Step Twelve, we strive to apply the spiritual principles of the Al-Anon program "in all our affairs"—including in our sexual relationships. In working on issues of trust, communication, and setting boundaries, we are already bringing spiritual principles into all other aspects of our relationships: Turning over our sexual relationships is just another way of doing the same thing. We can benefit from the comfort and guidance of a Higher Power in every aspect of our lives—including our sexuality—regardless of how worthy or unworthy that part of our lives may seem to us.

How we go about asking for a Higher Power's guidance in our lives is entirely up to us. There is no one solution to our common problem, no single action that will cure all ills. In Al-Anon, we are encouraged to find our own path of recovery. When others share their experience, strength and hope, we can, as it says in Al-Anon's Suggested Closing, "Take what you liked and leave the rest." We are free to determine for ourselves what we will and will not put into practice in our daily lives. Whatever is healing for us will contribute to our spiritual well-being.

Members Share Experience, Strength and Hope

Today I look for a positive spiritual payoff

My role models for sexual intimacy were based in my alcoholic family. My mother was a people-pleaser and this led to using her beautiful face and body to attract men and compete with women. She also changed who she was, based on who she was with at the time. I adopted relationship skills based on what I saw in her. I also isolated as a child, watching a lot of television. Rather than develop a sense of self, I practiced what I saw on television.

There were secrets, shame, criticism and judgment in my home. The disease conditioned me to believe that if I could make others happy, regardless of my well-being, then I would attract men and be loved. Looking for love and acceptance through sex became the basis for my self-esteem and confidence.

I did not have an identity as a child. I did not have a Higher Power until I started working the principles of Al-Anon. Through recovery, I have come to know myself. If I can become intimate with myself through knowing who I am and become intimate with my Higher Power through the Steps, Traditions and Concepts, I can be intimate with another human being.

Al-Anon has helped me to make decisions based on my best interests, based on the question "Do I want this?" and based on a positive spiritual payoff. I seek my Higher Power's will for me in all decisions, including having sex. God wants what is best for me. This includes having a healthy sexual relationship with a partner who is my spiritual equal, one with whom there is open and honest communication, trust and respect. I learned these spiritual values in Al-Anon.

Spiritual connection helped me have a healthy relationship

I was raised with the belief that other people were responsible for me. In most relationships, this meant that my self-worth was tied into what I believed other people thought about me. When it came to men, it meant that they were to take care of me financially. No one was taking care of my emotional needs. I was constantly putting myself in a position to be hurt as I expected and accepted degrading behavior from men and myself.

My first Al-Anon meeting was led by a woman who embodied serenity, although I was unable to label it at the time. About three months later she told her story and shared some aspects of her sexual past that resonated with me. I asked her to sponsor me. She and I began to work the Steps together. Through her behavior, I learned about self-respect, self-love, trust and intimacy. She also shared her humanness so that I did not make her into my Higher Power. It was the first healthy long-term relationship I had.

About a year into my recovery, I met a man. During our first date, we learned that we were both in recovery and we gave each other permission to discuss anything about the other with our Sponsors. I was ready and able to put my emotional health first. I continued to practice spiritual disciplines daily: prayer and meditation first thing each morning, daily Step work, conscious contact with my Higher Power throughout each day and staying connected with others in recovery through telephone calls, emails or meetings. Early in our relationship, I set boundaries for myself by making a call to an Al-Anon friend before I called him. It was important for me to maintain a sense of self.

Throughout the relationship, I continued to work the program and focus on my relationship with my Higher Power. It was important for me to have a balanced relationship with my partner, so we worked on connecting spiritually (praying and meditating together; discussing our beliefs), emotionally (sharing our feelings with each other and talking about our past experiences), and physically (hand holding, touching, kissing and other sexual acts).

There were times when I felt emotionally disturbed over the relationship; all of my insecurities came to the surface as we navigated a partnership in recovery. I knew that it would be detrimental if I relied on my partner to make me feel better. Instead I continued to seek comfort and peace from God. I was able to hold on loosely and let go gently, continuing to seek and follow spiritual guidance. The relationship was full of loving, tender moments and exceptional experiences. It was also full of challenges and opportunities to grow.

As the relationship with my partner grew, I learned how to practice healthy communication. It became clear that I had very wobbly boundaries for myself when it came to sexual acts. I took action by doing something different. I discussed the matter with my Sponsor and made a commitment that I would discuss specifics with her before I engaged in them. This act of self-love gave me an opportunity to act deliberately, and it also helped me to clarify what I wanted (and didn't want) before I took sexual actions. There was some discomfort as I spoke about certain sexual behaviors out loud to my Sponsor, but it was so healthy for me to be able to do so. In the past—despite what I claimed to value—I lacked integrity when it came to what I actually did. My Sponsor helped me to show myself respect. The relationship with my partner benefited from my sense of wholeness.

My Sponsor was also there when the relationship ended. I was able to respond with dignity and grace to my partner's decision to break up. I felt my feelings—mainly pain and sadness—and allowed myself the space to be present to them. *Opening Our Hearts, Transforming Our Losses* (B-29) helped me process my grief.

Because I had not made this man into my life and given over my emotional power, I knew that I would survive the loss and that I would move on to love again. I rested in God's loving care and continued to take care of myself by working the Steps and using the tools—including meetings for hugs, literature for clarity and validation, and my Sponsors and program friends for love and encouragement. I knew that I was not alone. It was a healthy end to a healthy relationship. Through working the Twelve Steps, I had gained a measure of emotional health which I carry with me into other relationships.

I don't have to force a solution

I am a young Al-Anon member who started off in Alateen nearly five years ago. Based on viewing my parents, who are still married, I felt like the best thing to hope for when finding a husband would be misery and hostility, since I saw plenty of it between them in their marriage. Based on my personal experience, I knew men to be manipulative, cruel, dishonest and unworthy of my time. Men were beneath the female gender! And yet, I also remember hoping and dreaming that there were men like those I saw in fairy tales or in the books with happy endings; real men who could be equal to women, however futile it was to hope for these things.

Currently I am casually dating two young men from A.A., which has brought up many fears and insecurities of mine about intimacy with men. Certain memories have come flooding back to me: being sexually assaulted by a boy I thought was a friend of mine on my high school campus; having a serious relationship with a man that fueled my sick symptom of enabling (by way of emotional manipulation through guilt!); being lulled to sleep some nights by my parents' yelling and fighting; and other such memories where I can now see, thanks to Al-Anon, that I cast myself as a victim.

These two young men in A.A. have both helped me in different ways. With one man, I have had a physically intimate encounter. He didn't manipulate me. He respected my boundaries and I felt like he showed me true compassion and tenderness in our embrace. This was a drastic shift from what I had previously experienced with other men. I felt no disgust, shame, victimization, or regret about our experience. In fact, I thank my Higher Power for giving me an opportunity and a friend to help me swallow my fears in order to pursue such an experience with such a worthy person. He and I are still friends. Our encounter didn't complicate our friendship; we discussed matters openly and agreed to continue our friendship. Neither one of us is ready to pursue a relationship at the present time.

As the other young man and I became better acquainted, he wanted to start a relationship with me. But he was looking for a healthy relationship and realized that I had many unresolved issues with men. We had a heated discussion that put a fire in my belly—desperation to resolve my issues. I did an Eleventh Step, and the meditation helped to cleanse me of the negativity around my past experiences with men. I was able to detach enough from those situations to forgive myself and even the men involved. I also was able to take comfort in knowing that both young men offered opportunities to show me that I did learn something from those past experiences. I learned how to move forward and not stay in a negative, self-perpetuated cycle of pity and shame.

Both of these young men were aware that I was only interested in casually dating, so they knew I wasn't dating just one person. However, a dilemma arose when I felt pressure from outside sources to choose one young man over the other. This led me to my old habit of people-pleasing and wanting the approval of these outside persons.

Steps Three and Eleven helped me the most with this. In the Third Step, I decide to turn my will and my life over to my Higher Power's care. To me, this means that I stay open to the wisdom and guidance that I can receive when I choose to communicate with my Higher Power. I consider Step Eleven as the action form of Step Three. I maintain constant contact with my Higher Power by praying and meditating. I am willing to let my Higher Power help me and I am meditating to put myself closer to the source from which the guidance is coming.

Eventually, I felt guided to let the situation unfold naturally. Talking with my Sponsor helped me understand what that meant. She said that if I am happy with where I am in relation to each young man, and if I have been honest and upfront with both of them about how I conduct myself, then maybe I was trying to force a choice where none was needed. I don't have to pick between the two of them—not yet anyway.

I am 20 years old, I am just now starting to enter the dating scene, and I want to have fun. I still have my guard up around men, but I am quick to retract my hostility when the man I am dealing with has given me no reason for alarm. My past is unchangeable, and I may regress into old patterns of thinking, but as long as I am willing to be guided by my Higher Power (Step Three) and maintain contact with my Higher Power (Step Eleven), I know that I will not stay in that unhealthy place for long.

I can turn intimacy over to my Higher Power

Growing up in a chaotic home as the result of the family disease of alcoholism, trust did not come easily. While I have made progress in other areas of my life, my marriage of 40 years is far from satisfactory. Many years ago, my husband and I managed my parents' business. One day, my father told me he did not trust me to run his financial affairs and shortly after that my employment ended. As a result, I have realized that I had a belief that I am not worthy of love or of being trusted. The bottom line was I could not possibly imagine what my husband could see to love and desire in me.

Step One tells me that I am powerless over intimacy and my life is unmanageable. I have given up trying to figure out what I can do to change things. If I could do that I wouldn't need Al-Anon. I now have only to turn this hurt over to my Higher Power, whom I choose to call God. I ask for His guidance and place my relationship in His hands. Whenever I can come from that place, my relationship is working and healing, little by little.

The gifts of the program were going off like fireworks

After eight years of recovery, everything changed in my attitude toward my husband. I went from not being willing to even consider trusting my newly recovering husband to being willing to follow him into the dark. We had a marriage based on recovery, so good it was beyond my wildest dreams. And then I had the awareness and acceptance that I am gay.

Ending this marriage was devastating. The awareness of my sexuality had nothing to do with the love I have in my heart for this man. We love each other very much. Thanks to Al-Anon, the process of ending our marriage was loving, thoughtful, courteous, respectful and kind. We lived together for months, and found a second home four doors down so our 11-year-old son could go back and forth freely. The gifts of the program went off like fireworks.

During this time my husband said to me, "Remember what Abraham Lincoln said: 'Most folks are as happy as they make up their minds to be.' We will be happy again. It's a choice. God brought us this far, He's not going to drop us now." I was thankful for the reminder. I knew there was no 'blame' to be placed, but I felt very responsible for what was happening. My heart ached daily for six years, but it was also full of joy and happiness. There is a plan. I'm so thankful I knew my feet were firmly planted on His path and I kept putting one foot in front of the other.

I needed to be a friend first and let God take care of the rest

After my first wife left me, I got into a number of unhealthy relationships with women. This was because my attitudes and actions with others still had not changed very much. In spite of being in Al-Anon for a while, I was still getting into dysfunctional relationships, and I still hadn't learned about letting go of what another person said, did or felt. I still kept on doing what I had been doing, which was trying to change each girlfriend into the kind of person I wanted her to be.

As I've heard around Al-Anon meetings, "You're getting what you're getting because you're doing what you're doing." That was me. But a moment of clarity came to me while I was having a solitary meal at my favorite Chinese restaurant. The God of my understanding has a sense of humor, and He answered my prayers in an unusual way. When I opened up the fortune cookie at the end of the meal, the fortune read: "If you would be loved, love and be loveable."

I finally got it! I had still been trying to force solutions, because I hadn't learned to genuinely "Let Go and Let God." I knew I had to change my old, unworkable attitudes towards relationships. At last, I realized that I needed to be a friend first and let the God of my understanding handle the rest. I tucked that fortune into my wallet as a reminder, which is still helpful to me today.

Then I got a once-in-a-lifetime opportunity to attend Al-Anon's first International Convention, concurrent with A.A.'s International Convention in Montreal, Canada. I could only get a room reservation on the outskirts of Montreal where the people only spoke French. My only French came from an English-French dictionary. And so I rented a car (to commute downtown to the Convention) and trusted God to help me with my language difficulties.

And who should come along to the same rural motel but two Al-Anon women from New York state, who also didn't speak French. They didn't have a way to get into the city for the Convention, so I suggested that we three commute into town and eat meals together. And God worked His miracles on me with these two ladies. Over the course of a week, we shared our stories together. At our last breakfast together at the end of the week, these

Al-Anon women gave me a little button with a red heart and an attached ribbon. It said: 100% loveable. (The fortune cookie saying was beginning to work!) I still treasure that button today, for it told me my life was changing for the better.

I left that Convention with a renewed vigor in my program. I got serious about working the Twelve Steps in my life with my Sponsor. I learned the Al-Anon axiom that "to keep it, I had to give it away." I learned about the Twelve Traditions and added some serious Al-Anon service commitments above group level. I also got an Al-Anon Service Sponsor. Then I began applying the Twelve Concepts of Service to my life as well. Each of these Al-Anon Legacies gave my personal growth a big boost. I learned about acceptance, about being a friend first, and I experienced firsthand how powerful my Higher Power is in real life, when I got out of His way.

Waiting for guidance kept me from needing to make amends

The intimate relationship with my husband was over. The love and trust were gone. The damage was done. The divorce was final. Acceptance was all that was left. I had a strong program and he had been in recovery for many years, so how did this happen? For once, I had chosen a recovering alcoholic and things were supposed to be wonderful—but they weren't, and I was so bothered by that fact. I came to realize that both our lives were still affected by this disease.

My Sponsor was so much a part of my life the months before and after our divorce. I felt so sad for the loss of a dream. Because of her loving support and guidance, I was able to get through this very difficult time without having to make amends for anything. I was able to practice saying what I meant, meaning what I said, but not saying it mean. We did a Fourth and Fifth Step on my marriage and I continually consulted my Higher Power. Finally, acceptance was realized!

After a year or so of little contact, my former husband and I ran into each other at a gas station. An issue came up and I investigated the situation. When I did, I realized things were not on the up and up. I found myself in the delightful position of having information with which to perhaps inflict some humorous revenge on my ex-husband. It seemed very harmless (to me, anyway) and I was going to get some pleasure out of listening to his outrage.

As has been my practice for quite some time, due to this program, I consulted my Higher Power before doing such acts, then waited for the peace to come and then move forward. The peace did not come, so I thought, "Well, maybe tomorrow." This went on for days and finally it was gone from my head.

Two or three weeks later, my ex-husband's oldest son committed suicide as a result of the disease of alcoholism. You can imagine how relieved I felt that I had not made that phone call. I knew what was going on several hours before he did, and the rest of his children were asking me to go be with him as soon as he was located. Some of my friends weren't too sure this was a good idea because of all that had happened over the past couple of years. I understood their concern, but I had clearly heard God say to me, "Take all the things you have inside you concerning him, and set them aside for now. I want you to show love and compassion."

Amazingly, I was able to do just that. My ex-husband showed up at my house that night and we cried and talked together. I helped gather information for his family as they had many decisions to make. I housed and fed other family members and helped them prepare for the celebration of my stepson's life. I was able to be of service to his family. God did for me what I could not do for myself.

The miracle of this whole experience is that all those things inside of me—that for some reason I was hanging on to—were gone, and God has never given them back to me.

Today, several years later, we are still good friends. We care about each other and love each other. We do not have a sexual relationship, but it is an intimate relationship. We realize it is best for both of us to not be married to each other, and we are both exactly where we are supposed to be. Life is much more enjoyable and peaceful this way for each of us. It would never have occurred to me that this would even be possible, but when I "Let Go and Let God," amazing things happen!

The spiritual meaning of intimacy

Through Al-Anon I learned the spiritual meaning of intimacy in my marriage. For me, intimacy is the ability to honestly share my feelings, insights and experiences without fear of criticism or judgment. I am safe to be me.

Spiritual intimacy is created when I invite my Higher Power into my daily life. My husband and I join hands and pray out loud every day for God to be the center of our marriage. We have celebrated ten years of marriage, with both of us in recovery, each of us working our own programs. As we get older, physical changes and "indignities" alter our outside bodies, but the spiritual dimensions blossom and flourish.

The slogan "How Important Is It?" reminds me of what I value most in my relationship. The sweetness of sharing my innermost feelings and dreams is irreplaceable. That ability to share—that intimacy—is a blessing.

The tools are already at my disposal

I believe in a Higher Power, and I also believe I've seen His work. However, I have the hardest time turning to my Higher

Power first and then thanking Him later. I always want to take care of the situation myself, and not ask for help. Then I am exhausted, angry, anxious and generally unpleasant for anyone to be around. So many times it takes the Al-Anon literature, my Sponsor or my husband—or all three!—to remind me to turn it over to God. It's not anything I can control, so I need to let it go and take care of myself—the one thing I can control.

I struggle with and feel guilty about this "deficient" relationship I have with my Higher Power. The guilt is probably leftover from my religious upbringing, but the struggle is very real. Step Three ("Made a decision to turn our will and our lives over to the care of God *as we understood Him*") has helped, but I need more. I have begun working past Step Three, but I still find myself talking with my Sponsor about the continuing menace of self-will.

What do I want? A peace in knowing that I can turn to my Higher Power and then the ability to actually do it. Then it occurred to me: I have done this before! I did it when I worked Step Three, I just need to keep doing it. Amazingly enough, the tools are at my disposal.

I need to connect with my Higher Power and with myself

I have a great need to share who I am with another human being who accepts my human weaknesses; someone without expectations that I will change, improve, do things the "right" way or even recover; someone who has time for me; and someone who "lights up" when they see me. To me, this is intimacy.

I have been reminded in Al-Anon to seek an intimate relationship with my Higher Power rather than frantically searching for an intimate relationship with a person. I wondered how to do that. It came to me that a relationship is built by spending time together. A relationship can become intimate when two beings spend time together, listen to each other and feel safe to share honestly.

Now, I want to spend time with my Higher Power. I talk to Him throughout the day. I ask for guidance, for strength to do His will but I also tell Him how I feel and what I think. I thank Him for help in uncomfortable situations. I ask Him what to buy at the store and what to wear in the morning.

It also occurred to me that I need to have an intimate relationship with myself! I can spend time getting to know myself through journaling. The more time I spend getting to know all aspects of me, the easier it becomes for the "committee" in my head to begin to work together, cooperating for our common good.

All of my relationships are in my Higher Power's hands

I'm a single woman, and have been since I started recovery over three years ago. I am learning in Al-Anon the importance of emotional intimacy and taking my time to really know a man before being physically intimate. It's a process and sometimes a challenge, but overall I'm proud of my progress. I'm learning to date in a healthy way.

Before Al-Anon, my sexuality was a source of shame for me. Due to early childhood experiences, I learned to associate sexual feelings with abuse, abandonment and secrecy. One of my biggest fears in beginning Al-Anon was that I'd have to share my secrets and face the painful feelings associated with telling them. I felt it would eventually be part of my healing process and it terrified me—so much so that, at times, I felt like running away and hiding, as I had when I was afraid as a small child.

But at those times my Higher Power was with me, encouraging me to be patient, gentle and compassionate with myself, to trust that things would unfold when and as they were meant to, as I was ready. "Slow and steady, as I feel ready" is the approach I took, especially when it came time for Step Four ("Made a searching and fearless moral inventory of ourselves"). That is where most of my fear accumulated, turning Step Four into something that looked more like a monster than a spiritual tool to help me grow.

Again, my Higher Power was with me, continuing to encourage patience, gentleness and compassion. I think people who have experienced abuse have a greater capacity to abuse themselves, so going at a slow pace and loving myself as my Higher Power loves me was integral for me. I took "fearless" inventory to mean that I don't have to be afraid. I can take as long as I need to on each Step, praying, trusting and following my Higher Power the entire way. Like a light that goes on before me, illuminating the shadows and false fears, my Higher Power gives me courage and shows me the truth.

My Higher Power led me to a Fourth Step group that followed a pace that felt comfortable to me. As we progressed through Al-Anon's *Blueprint for Progress* (P-91), I was able to build a sense of trust and emotional intimacy in the group. I was also building trust and emotional intimacy with my Sponsor. I learned that healthy, loving relationships take time to build. And I shared my secrets as I felt ready to do so, receiving love and acceptance in return.

I always pray for guidance, especially before revealing something personal. I wait until I feel a "yes" or "no" from my Higher Power. Sometimes I get a "no" and I trust that. It's okay. The timing or situation may not be right, or I may just not feel ready. This is one of the ways I take care of myself, get closer to my Higher Power, and get to know myself.

Establishing a sense of intimacy, for me, starts with a close, intimate relationship with my Higher Power. From that foundation of strength, I get to know my true self, without all the baggage and fear. From that place, I am able to be honest and intimate with others.

I haven't dated much in recovery, but I have found that my Higher Power brings people into my life to teach me about how I behave in relationships. I feel as though my Higher Power is preparing me and healing me to continue to learn about and develop healthy relationships—romantic or otherwise— in the future, as I'm ready.

For now, I feel happy with where I am, being single. I really enjoy the extra time I have to spend with my Higher Power and myself, in peaceful solitude, as well as with others. I find it very nurturing and fulfilling. My Higher Power is my refuge, sustaining me through life's storms and celebrating with me through the victories. The greatest gift I have received from Al-Anon is my strong faith and my loving, intimate relationship with my Higher Power.

Perhaps someday, if and when I am ready, my Higher Power will bring a romantic relationship into my life. I will continue to follow the approach with that relationship as I do with the rest of my life, working the Steps, with a specific focus on Steps One through Three. All of my relationships are in my Higher Power's hands, where they belong. I trust in my Higher Power's will, wisdom and knowledge more than my limited understanding.

Questions for Reflection

1. In what ways do I feel connected to others? To a Higher Power? To myself?

2. Which Al-Anon tools have helped improve my relationships? How?

3. Which Al-Anon tools have I not implemented in my recovery? What is preventing me from using them?

4. What actions do I take when I feel isolated or alone? What are the results of these actions?

5. Which relationships in my life are the most difficult to turn over to a Higher Power's care?

6. In which relationships do I find it easier to "Let Go and Let God"?

7. What is my relationship with a Higher Power like? How is it similar to relationships with other people? How is it different?

8. In what areas of my life do I feel comfortable asking for a Higher Power's guidance? In what areas of my life is this idea uncomfortable to me?

9. Have I turned over my sex life to my Higher Power? If not, is there anything that is blocking me from doing that?

10. What things do I do that I consider to be spiritual practices?

Chapter Six
Expressing Gratitude

As we continue to grow in the Al-Anon program, we gradually make more room for close, intimate relationships in our lives. The more we practice the principles of the Al-Anon program in those relationships, the more we come to feel that closeness—to ourselves, our Higher Power, and other people in our lives—no matter what kind of relationship we may have with them. We may not get precisely the kind of intimacy we were looking for, but we can enjoy intimacy in our lives nonetheless, as these Al-Anon members share:

- "Though I do not have sexual or physical intimacy in my life right now, I can still foster joyful, honest, safe relationships with the special people in my life."

- "I had to let go of having my desires fulfilled in a certain way, and when I did, I could begin receiving the love that was offered in Al-Anon meetings."

- "Al-Anon has given me friendship, hugs, a hand squeeze when I'm down, and real live people to talk to at meetings and on the phone."

- "As I recover through the program, sex now seems very connected to deep, emotional intimacy—and consistent, reliable intimacy at that."

- "I felt like I could never hug my parents because it had never happened. The idea was uncomfortable because it was so unfamiliar. But Al-Anon showed me how to express love to people. I watched people take turns to talk, help each other, and most of all, hug one another. Experiencing that gave me an idea of how to show love to someone. During one of my next visits home after attending Al-Anon for a few months, I was able to express my love to my family and hug them."

- "Sex and intimacy involve complex emotions. Being comfortable with my human emotions has really freed me to enjoy giving and receiving pleasure."

- "I've come a long way since I thought intimacy was simply a more formal and poetic synonym for sex. Nowadays, I think of the word as a synonym for real closeness, where 'real' doesn't just mean 'genuine'—it means 'honestly being who you are.' In this definition, sex is an optional part of what I now see as a much greater whole."

- "Al-Anon helped me see my husband as a child of God, who has good qualities and less desirable qualities, just like me. I learned to love him for who he is, not who I wanted him to be. I nurtured this new attitude by becoming more loving and attentive, giving more hugs, instigating some fun times, listening to him and valuing what he had to say. Gradually he responded in kind, and our relationship blossomed."

- "I suddenly remembered and was flooded with many good memories about my father. I wrote them down and put them into calligraphy, framed it and gave it to him, and now our relationship has really changed. When he does those 'alcoholic' things, our conversation is completely different."

When we get to experience the feelings of closeness, connectedness and trust, we may find ourselves wanting to express those feelings to the people in our lives. Although our loved ones may not always be able to accept words of love and gratitude, there are many ways we can let them know how we feel. Offering or accepting help, spending time together, taking time to listen without criticism, respecting others' boundaries, and showing appreciation for the little things people do for us are all ways to show those we love that we are grateful for their presence in our lives.

In relation to a Higher Power, expressions of gratitude may look a little different. Taking time to enjoy our surroundings, savoring a moment of peaceful contemplation, or simply saying "thank you" in a prayer are all ways of sharing our feelings of appreciation with the God of our understanding.

Most of all, gratitude is a gift we give ourselves. Cultivating an appreciation for the good things in our lives—no matter what else we may also experience—can help us to maintain our serenity through whatever life may bring us.

Members Share Experience, Strength and Hope

I had to let intimacy grow

When alcoholism began wrecking our marriage, I felt cheated—cheated out of a loved one's companionship. Many nights when my wife drank too much, I would lie awake next to her, wishing for the intimacy and pillow talk of years gone by. She frequently passed out not long after dinner, and I felt desperately lonely even with a house full of kids. While I believed there was some program that might one day help her, I never sought help for myself. I felt worse and worse with every passing month. I resigned myself to a cold, empty marriage, without physical intimacy or a life partner.

When I first learned in Al-Anon about letting go and detachment, I applied it with cold self-righteousness. I remained angry, touchy and moody. Later, I learned to apply it with love, and slowly learned that there was dignity for both me and my wife when I let certain events, crises and consequences occur. I learned to set and enforce boundaries about my house and drinking, but also learned to deal with the guilt that arose when I enforced boundaries. For a long time, my wife told me Al-Anon had made me cruel and heartless. Deep down, I agreed with her, although I kept my feelings to myself. Only through working my program and reasoning things out with a Sponsor did I overcome these feelings of guilt. I acted with self-confidence, but also with love—love for her, but also love for myself, as I changed my focus from the alcoholic to my own spiritual growth.

Working the Steps with my Sponsor boiled a lot of my problems down to one question: Had my cajoling, manipulations, and controlling behavior led her to stop drinking? No, I admitted. And yet, when I stopped all that, focused on myself and let go and let God into my life, my wife recognized her problem and got help. I take no credit; she has worked long and hard for her sobriety.

We will celebrate our 30th wedding anniversary this year. We have been through many troubles, and we continue to work our own programs. But lately, we have both recognized that intimacy is back in our marriage. We hold hands more. We express thanks and kindnesses with each other more often. We enjoy dinner out with the kids, and we talk about books and movies we both like. We read together in bed and exchange tender touches.

I believe intimacy is not so much achieved as it is grown. God grew it again in me when I allowed it to happen. The intimacy that I had craved when she was drinking is now growing again between us, and the loneliness has long faded.

My home group showed me real intimacy

There was a man standing inside the door greeting people as I arrived at my first Al-Anon meeting. His welcome was warm and kind. He and I started dating after a year and we both have that same home group five years later. I learned to love him and his family, especially his son, a sweet young man who was his reason for joining Al-Anon. He and I watched as his son catapulted through life. A month ago, he got the call that most of us dread. His beloved son had died suddenly from his disease.

It was a Sunday night, and sometime the next day I shot off an email and text messages to our program friends to share the sad news. Despite our sadness, and also because of it, Monday night we both were at our home group meeting.

It was amazing to see what happened. Member after member arrived, filling the room. What was usually a group of about 40 folks swelled to over 60. People hugged him, and I could feel the heartache in the room. The Chairperson handed me a reading and when I realized it was the Suggested Closing, my heart sank. The Closing is my favorite reading and the closest to my spirit. How could I read it tonight? But my grieving partner sat on one side and a newcomer on the other, so I could not pass it on to anyone else.

The members' sharings were intense and moving. I could feel the room growing heavy with grief. Eventually it was time for my reading and my eyes filled with tears. Everyone was looking at me, but I couldn't speak for a minute.

There was a palpable hush in the room as I finally, haltingly, began. I deliberately read slowly and as I got to, "Whatever your problems, there are those among us who have had them, too," my tears fell. I stumbled on to, "You will come to realize that there is no situation too difficult to be bettered and no unhappiness too great to be lessened," and I heard others sniffling, too.

It took a while for me to get to the end, and as I read, "let the understanding, love, and peace of the program grow in you one day at a time," I looked up and almost everyone was crying.

You see, this young man was not just my partner's son, he was a son to all of us in that meeting. We all lost him. This was the most intimate moment I have ever felt in a meeting. It was collective suffering. This was intimacy at its deepest and most heartfelt, and something I will never forget. The fellowship continues to embrace my partner and me during this sad time, and it is the hope we find in Al-Anon that is getting us through.

Intimate moments can happen anywhere

A friend's 1940s vintage car sat in the parking lot of a meeting I attend regularly. It reminded me of the gangster cars from the old movies: black, sleek and beautiful. I had been feeling pretty low that week, and after the meeting, my friend invited me to go for a ride. The music on the radio was also from that time period. It was a perfect setting.

As we traveled, other drivers beeped their horns. Other passengers waved. I found myself smiling and waving back. At one point, I realized that my dear friend and I were sharing an intimate moment. He was fully engaged in driving the vehicle and all that entailed, and I was fully enjoying being a passenger—smiling, waving and sightseeing along the way. We were viewing this shared experience in different ways. Each of us walked away with a different memory.

Al-Anon taught me that these moments can be anywhere, anytime and with anyone. Sometimes, these moments happen only with my Higher Power. When I got into my own car to drive home, I no longer felt low. Thank you, Al-Anon, for making me aware of the moments that mean so much.

Gratitude helped me find healthy intimacy

Being a gay man and coming from an alcoholic home, I have particular challenges of being intimate. Knowing only what I had learned from my family of origin, I first created an alcoholic marriage with a woman that lasted 17 years. Later I created an alcoholic partnership with a man that lasted two. Thus, in early recovery, it was easy for me to admit that I was intimacy-challenged.

When I entered Al-Anon, a Sponsor suggested I first write a gratitude list of all the intimate relationships in my life that did not have to do with romance. I was amazed at the result. I had many, many close ties which I had just not seen. For example, there was a woman with whom I shared running regimens, a married couple with whom I went on outings and a next-door neighbor with whom I shared holidays as well as a love of flowers. This list served as a fallback, a way of saying that I was fine being single. It was also a launching point to a long, 20-year period of dating. Settled in a spirit of gratitude about the intimate relationships already in my life, I did not have to force a solution in the form of getting an instantaneous husband.

In the years following, I dated perhaps 300 to 400 men over a period of two decades. The date could be dinner, coffee, or a sustained time of intimate acquaintance, including lovemaking. Always I tried to stay out of the bars, since they were the places where I had formerly done what I call "albatross hunting"—that is, looking for a man I could hang as a caretaking burden around my neck: a thoroughly dysfunctional man, probably a practicing alcoholic, who would only weigh me down and eventually turn away, thus "saving" me again from real intimacy.

Throughout all my dates, I worked to follow the spiritual formula: "Say what I feel, ask for what I want, let go of the results, and come to know what I need to know." This formula was especially important when mustering up the courage to call a man up and ask him out on a date—something an older man generally did not do in our gay community. It was also important when being clear about the kind of safe sex I wanted. All in all, this form of dating gave me practice in developing intimacy, helping me to trust the process and let go of outcomes. My Sponsor kept telling me that when I went out for coffee with a man, just have coffee. The date didn't have to be a springboard to marriage to be valuable.

I am very grateful for all the talented, intelligent, good-look-ing, and funny men who agreed to date me and who became a part of my life. I enjoyed sex on a usually monogamous basis, and as a means of getting to know myself and my friend better. However, over the years, I always found a point where the rela-tionship seemed to come to a standstill. Sometimes this discov-ery included the disclosure that the man was an alcoholic or an untreated family member of an alcoholic after all. In applying the Al-Anon principle of not trying to change others, I was able then to discover how much time I wanted to spend with him. Eventually the irreconcilable differences meant we needed to part company as lovers. Also, I made a pledge to myself that if I could see plainly down the road that the man was not someone I could "marry," then it was time to stop having sex. Otherwise remaining physically intimate, when all spiritual intimacy had stopped, would simply be further cause for heartbreak.

After 20 years of dating, I met a man with long-term sobri-ety who would eventually become my life partner. However, our initial times together were not particularly compatible, and we stopped seeing each other. I was not yet ready for full intimacy, and neither was he. Six years later, we met again, and soon dated exclusively. We have been together now for over six years, and share a home and life together. At first I wanted to buy a duplex together and live separate but adjoining lives. However, with the prompting of my partner, eventually I accepted the full challenge of living in recovery with him under the same roof.

Because I am still not highly proficient at intimacy, and since my partner is a recovering alcoholic, it is especially important for me to keep up with my Al-Anon program. I try to have a good day no matter what kind he is having, and I still try to apply the principle of "Say how I feel, ask for what I want, let go of the results, and come to know what I need to know" when we are in conversation. Each morning, we try to check in with each other and discuss what is happening in our lives, especially in the area of our feelings. Finally, I still try to have other intimate, non-romantic relationships in my life which, of course, include a Sponsor, so that my soul mate remains my partner and does not become my Higher Power.

My motives made all the difference

I love the bluebells that bloom at a nearby park in April. I go to see them almost every spring because the expanse of bluebells and other wildflowers along the flowing creek in the bare forest is, to me, almost magical.

One spring I invited a friend to go with me. The bluebells were at their vibrant peak—so beautiful!—and we had such a good time that a thought entered my mind: My husband would enjoy seeing those bluebells. My next thought was the reality: My husband was an active alcoholic and this late in the afternoon he would be already staggering drunk, which would be obvious and embarrassing, as the bluebell path was a popular one.

I decided the bluebells were too beautiful to miss. I went back home, and he let me drive him to see the bluebells. After the walk he thanked me for bringing him. It was an intimate time, enjoying nature together.

My husband died about two years later of the disease. You can bet that I savor such nice memories of us together, and that bit of kindness I was able to offer him. I had not suggested the walk to "fix" his alcoholism, but Al-Anon and the bluebells had elevated my motives to where I could simply enjoy the time with my husband, whether he was drinking or not.

If strangers could show compassion, so could I

In the same way that my wife's alcoholism has progressed, both physical and emotional intimacy have progressively left our marriage. The only time there is any sexual contact is when she is drinking. There is very little sexual activity at all. The worst part of living with this disease is the lack of emotional intimacy. The simple act of holding hands or hugging each other is practically nonexistent and this part hurts even more.

In the four months since I came to Al-Anon, I've taken a close look at myself and discovered I have been emotionally unavailable to my wife. How could I expect her to be close to me if I wasn't willing to be close to her? How could I expect sexual contact when I was unavailable myself? I was not emotionally available throughout the marriage even before the alcoholism had progressed. For years, I've put the absence of a sex life and emotional closeness entirely on my alcoholic, but now I know I've played a big part in the lack of intimacy in my marriage.

This new awareness started for me at an Al-Anon convention. In my entire life I've never been hugged by so many people I didn't know. It showed me that if others that didn't know me could show such compassion, so could I.

This look in the mirror through Al-Anon has given me slow but steady results. I'm expressing my feelings to my alcoholic. I've stated that I have not been emotionally available throughout the marriage. I've expressed a desire to be held, to hold hands with her and for us to connect with each other.

It's slow progress and that's okay. We're holding hands again, we're telling each other we love each other again, we're more available to each other. I am emotionally available to my wife. There was little hope and fleeting love before Al-Anon, but now? There is hope. There is love.

I can appreciate our differences

My favorite way to unwind at home is to lie down in bed for 10 to 20 minutes. It allows me to mentally process the multiple tasks I have been working on, let them go and clear my mind for a fresh start on things when I get up.

The other day, my husband came in the bedroom while I was unwinding. I invited him to relax with me. He said, "Okay." Then he noticed that something was wrong with the ceiling fan over the bed. He went out to the garage and came back with a ladder and tools. While I was trying to unwind, he was up on a ladder over the bed, working on the ceiling fan. At first I felt a bit annoyed. Then I laughed, "This is not very relaxing—for me!" He laughed, too, and came down from the ladder to give me a kiss. Then he got back up on the ladder to continue working on the ceiling fan.

As I smiled up at my husband, I thought about how far we have come since I started attending Al-Anon. Some months ago, we would have ended up talking about this at a marriage counselor's office. I imagined the counselor telling me, "Don't you think you could appreciate your husband for fixing the fan right away instead of putting it off for weeks?" And to him, "Don't you think you could find a more courteous time to fix the ceiling fan?" Instead, we both had a good laugh at the absurdity of me lying in the bed "complaining" that it was not relaxing for me to watch him work!

Through Al-Anon, I have come to understand him better as a person, separate from me, with his own point of view and his own way of doing things. I appreciate the good things he brings to the marriage even more now. I see my previous flaw of wanting to direct how and when he does things. Al-Anon principles are helping me to squelch this most annoying habit.

My husband appreciates me so much these days! He appreciates what I contribute to running the household. He appreciates me when I respond with a sense of humor instead of irritation. And he appreciates the fact that I appreciate him and don't try to control him.

Thank you, Al-Anon!

I had no idea how completely my feelings could change

Forgiveness was a destination I'd never thought was possible, or even desirable, to reach. I grew up with an alcoholic father. I learned fear and loathing through my interactions with him. Physically, he was a big, heavy-handed guy with a booming voice. In my child's mind, he was a brooding, hulking tyrant. He could be extremely argumentative and competitive. He demanded I know things that were beyond my years. His impatience and disappointment often resulted in harsh words. I saw nothing good about Dad. I often thought: *Why was I given such a horrible father?*

My secret was that I felt bad like my daddy—a little worse all the time. I became more withdrawn as I reached adolescence, never talking very much—especially not to him. Eventually, the dam of shame and self-hatred burst. When I was 21, I got drunk and threw up at an Independence Day party. I vaguely remember my parents carrying me home. All the while, I kept saying that I hated myself and wanted to die. I felt so ashamed of what happened.

Shortly after this incident, my father went into rehab again. It turned out to be for the last time. Although we never discussed it, I believe that seeing his son in such incredible pain finally pierced through his denial. Dad finally reached sobriety. Early in his recovery, he encouraged my brother and me to get into Al-Anon. He, and my mom, too, made amends for their abuse and neglect. It took six years until I was ready (and in enough pain) to commit to recovery. What blessings have occurred since then!

When my dad had a near-fatal illness, it was a wake-up call for me. I'd wanted to tell him that I'd forgiven him but still didn't feel ready, so I knew what I had to work on. My mom and dad were living in a beach house on a North Carolina barrier island. Some of my happiest memories of them are in that house. It finally felt like we were a loving family. This gave me the willingness to tell my dad that I'd forgiven him.

Sadly, Dad got cancer a few years later. They moved to Florida. To be honest, for all these years, I'd never completely trusted that Dad would remain sober. When he got sick, I thought he would go back to drinking for sure. He never did, though. If anything was going to do it, you'd think it would have been that. In fact, I think his compulsion had already been lifted by his Higher Power. I am forever grateful!

When it became apparent that my dad was terminally ill, I decided to visit. I got to spend time with him and help with his care. It was one of the best decisions I have ever made. During that time, I felt such tenderness and fondness for him as did he for me. As a boy, I could never have imagined how completely my feelings toward him would change. I actually saw him as a trusted friend. I'm so thankful I could let go of my anger and hatred while he was still living.

Thanks to our shared journey of recovery, that ugly picture of my dad had been wiped away. I now saw him as a human being. Although we're very different men, I could see our common traits and shared family history. Who would have dreamed that I'd honestly enjoy my dad's company? It's an Al-Anon miracle, really!

My Higher Power provided a chance to heal

A few years after my husband's death, I started seeing someone new. I was nervous, excited and wary. I attended an Area-sponsored weekend event in the mountains, and shared this news with many of my friends. One of the workshops that weekend was on intimacy, and I laughingly decided to attend. I thought I would talk about this new relationship. My Higher Power had other ideas.

As I listened to others share, I kept thinking about the last year of my husband's life. He was an alcoholic and we had been married 21 years. At one point he had over four years of sobriety in A.A., and we shared a lot of happy times. Then he became addicted to pain medication and illegal drugs, and started drinking again. Al-Anon was extremely important to me as I felt I had lost my best friend when he stopped going to meetings or taking part in events. We had separated briefly a few years before his death, and our relationship was strained at best. Our intimate life was nonexistent.

In a new job and feeling overwhelmed, I asked for my husband's help. We ended up working together and we travelled a lot to various job-related sites. Some trips were strained, while others were filled with conversations and sharing by both of us. We told each other stories, laughed about our granddaughter's antics, and I felt more connected to him than I had in a long time.

On the last trip we took together, we both really opened up about our lives. We shared information about friends, events and feelings. The drive was six hours long, but it was filled with talk, laughter and a lot of "I didn't know that!" from both of us. He was leaving me at an Al-Anon member's house so I could travel with her to an Al-Anon event out of state. When he got ready to leave, I gave him a huge hug and kiss, told him "I do love you" and said goodbye. That was the last time I saw him. He died in a car accident on the way home.

What I realized and shared with the group in that intimacy workshop was that God had provided us with a way to reconnect. We were closer than we had been and were moving forward. I was given that year to heal and find the man I loved once again. Just knowing that we said goodbye on good terms—with no arguments or blame or anger—made the grief over his death easier to deal with. We had found a form of intimacy that I often forget about: sharing our lives with each other.

I don't keep score anymore

At this point with my alcoholic mother, intimacy and communication are difficult—the rule of the house seems to be "see no evil, hear no evil, speak no evil." She wants to be left alone to drink herself into oblivion. The rest of the house is expected to adhere to her unspoken rule.

When I first returned home, I was reacting, taking things very personally and not detaching—I was miserable—until I began practicing the tools of Al-Anon. Before Al-Anon, I would be angry, not speak to her or tally up yet another offense.

Now I'm not keeping score anymore. Today, there is no yesterday—I'm taking it "One Day at a Time." When the house is filled with tension, negative feelings or the alcoholic's anger at everything, I refuse to engage. I get busy outside the home until the storm passes.

I must take care of my spiritual life daily in order to see and appreciate those moments, accepting that behind the mask of alcoholism is the mom I love. Accepting that I cannot get her sober, that only she can make that journey, allows me to mind my business, encourage her good qualities, allow her to have her dignity and give her respect even though she is slowly dying from this disease.

By practicing acceptance of her disease, I can love my mother or love around her. In quiet before the drinking starts, we can have intimate moments. Our shared interests in gardening, flowers and cooking is where I've learned to find the intimacy of honest communication, laughter and hope.

Questions for Reflection

1. Which relationships am I most grateful to have in my life today? Why?

2. In what ways has working the Al-Anon program changed my outlook on life?

3. What changes have I experienced that have brought me closer to those I love?

4. How connected do I feel to other members of the Al-Anon fellowship?

5. In which relationships do I feel most safe to be myself? Why?

6. What kinds of intimacy do I enjoy today? On which relationships do I rely for that intimacy?

7. How do I express gratitude for others in my life?

8. In what ways do I practice gratitude for my Higher Power? For myself and my recovery?

Epilogue

Practicing Intimacy

As the experience of our fellow Al-Anon members demonstrates, the more we practice Al-Anon's spiritual principles in all of our relationships, the more those relationships change. More than that, we change. As we build trust in ourselves and others, we begin to move through our lives with more confidence and less fear. By learning healthy ways to express ourselves and developing the ability to listen, we build connections with others, ourselves, and our Higher Power. In taking responsibility for our own needs, we become better able to see that those needs are met. With a solid spiritual foundation and the loving support of the Al-Anon fellowship, we find ourselves better equipped to be more fully ourselves, and to live more fulfilling lives.

Twelve Steps

Study of these Steps is essential to progress in the Al-Anon program. The principles they embody are universal, applicable to everyone, whatever his personal creed. In Al-Anon, we strive for an ever-deeper understanding of these Steps, and pray for the wisdom to apply them to our lives.

1. We admitted we were powerless over alcohol—that our lives had become unmanageable.

2. Came to believe that a Power greater than ourselves could restore us to sanity.

3. Made a decision to turn our will and our lives over to the care of God *as we understood Him.*

4. Made a searching and fearless moral inventory of ourselves.

5. Admitted to God, to ourselves, and to another human being the exact nature of our wrongs.

6. Were entirely ready to have God remove all these defects of character.

7. Humbly asked Him to remove our shortcomings.

8. Made a list of all persons we had harmed, and became willing to make amends to them all.

9. Made direct amends to such people wherever possible, except when to do so would injure them or others.

10. Continued to take personal inventory and when we were wrong promptly admitted it.

11. Sought through prayer and meditation to improve our conscious contact with God *as we understood Him*, praying only for knowledge of His will for us and the power to carry that out.

12. Having had a spiritual awakening as the result of these steps, we tried to carry this message to others, and to practice these principles in all our affairs.

Twelve Traditions

These guidelines are the means of promoting harmony and growth in Al-Anon groups and in the worldwide fellowship of Al-Anon as a whole. Our group experience suggests that our unity depends upon our adherence to these Traditions:

1. Our common welfare should come first; personal progress for the greatest number depends upon unity.

2. For our group purpose there is but one authority—a loving God as He may express Himself in our group conscience. Our leaders are but trusted servants—they do not govern.

3. The relatives of alcoholics, when gathered together for mutual aid, may call themselves an Al-Anon Family Group, provided that, as a group, they have no other affiliation. The only requirement for membership is that there be a problem of alcoholism in a relative or friend.

4. Each group should be autonomous, except in matters affecting another group or Al-Anon or AA as a whole.

5. Each Al-Anon Family Group has but one purpose: to help families of alcoholics. We do this by practicing the Twelve Steps of AA *ourselves*, by encouraging and understanding our alcoholic relatives, and by welcoming and giving comfort to families of alcoholics.

6. Our Family Groups ought never endorse, finance or lend our name to any outside enterprise, lest problems of money, property and prestige divert us from our primary spiritual aim. Although a separate entity, we should always co-operate with Alcoholics Anonymous.

7. Every group ought to be fully self-supporting, declining outside contributions.

8. Al-Anon Twelfth Step work should remain forever non-professional, but our service centers may employ special workers.

9. Our groups, as such, ought never be organized; but we may create service boards or committees directly responsible to those they serve.

10. The Al-Anon Family Groups have no opinion on outside issues; hence our name ought never be drawn into public controversy.

11. Our public relations policy is based on attraction rather than promotion; we need always maintain personal anonymity at the level of press, radio, films, and TV. We need guard with special care the anonymity of all AA members.

12. Anonymity is the spiritual foundation of all our Traditions, ever reminding us to place principles above personalities.

Twelve Concepts of Service

The Twelve Steps and Traditions are guides for personal growth and group unity. The Twelve Concepts are guides for service. They show how Twelfth Step work can be done on a broad scale and how members of a World Service Office can relate to each other and to the groups, through a World Service Conference, to spread Al-Anon's message worldwide.

1. The ultimate responsibility and authority for Al-Anon world services belongs to the Al-Anon groups.

2. The Al-Anon Family Groups have delegated complete administrative and operational authority to their Conference and its service arms.

3. The right of decision makes effective leadership possible.

4. Participation is the key to harmony.

5. The rights of appeal and petition protect minorities and insure that they be heard.

6. The Conference acknowledges the primary administrative responsibility of the Trustees.

7. The Trustees have legal rights while the rights of the Conference are traditional.

8. The Board of Trustees delegates full authority for routine management of Al-Anon Headquarters to its executive committees.

9. Good personal leadership at all service levels is a necessity. In the field of world service the Board of Trustees assumes the primary leadership.

10. Service responsibility is balanced by carefully defined service authority and double-headed management is avoided.

11. The World Service Office is composed of selected committees, executives and staff members.

12. The spiritual foundation for Al-Anon's world services is contained in the General Warranties of the Conference, Article 12 of the Charter.

General Warranties of the Conference

In all proceedings the World Service Conference of Al-Anon shall observe the spirit of the Traditions:

1. that only sufficient operating funds, including an ample reserve, be its prudent financial principle;

2. that no Conference member shall be placed in unqualified authority over other members;

3. that all decisions be reached by discussion vote and whenever possible by unanimity;

4. that no Conference action ever be personally punitive or an incitement to public controversy;

5. that though the Conference serves Al-Anon it shall never perform any act of government; and that like the fellowship of Al-Anon Family Groups which it serves, it shall always remain democratic in thought and action.

Intimacy in Alcoholic Relationships